Ira David Sankey

Christian Endeavor Hymns

Ira David Sankey

Christian Endeavor Hymns

ISBN/EAN: 9783337083472

Printed in Europe, USA, Canada, Australia, Japan

Cover: Foto ©Thomas Meinert / pixelio.de

More available books at **www.hansebooks.com**

CHRISTIAN ENDEAVOR

HYMNS

BY

IRA D. SANKEY

PUBLISHED BY

UNITED SOCIETY OF CHRISTIAN ENDEAVOR

646 Washington Street, Boston, Mass.

THE BIGLOW & MAIN CO.

76 EAST 9TH ST., NEW YORK.   215 WABASH AVE., CHICAGO.

PREFACE.

THIS volume of **Christian Endeavor Hymns** has been compiled at the urgent request of the United Society of Christian Endeavor, Boston, in response to many requests for a new C. E. Hymn Book especially adapted to the needs of the Society.

In addition to the large number of NEW HYMNS AND TUNES contained in this collection, there will also be found a valuable selection of useful and popular Gospel Songs and Standard Hymns.

We trust that these Sacred Songs, both old and new, may prove acceptable, and add fresh interest to the Service of Praise wherever used.

Ira D. Sankey

CHRISTIAN ENDEAVOR

HYMNS.

1   Help us to Worship Thee.

F. J. CROSBY.   IRA D. SANKEY.

1. Help us to wor-ship Thee, Sav-iour di - vine; Ear-ly to
2. Help us to hon - or Thee, Sav-iour and King, Gifts to Thy
3. Thou art the Ho - ly One, we are but dust, In Thine al -

fol - low Thee, our hearts in - cline; O make Thy pre - cious word,
al - tar, Lord, help us to bring; Ev - er to live for Thee,
might-y arm still may we trust; Help us to rev-'rence Thee,

day un - to day, Light to our way-ward feet, guiding our way.
Thy praise to speak; This be our mis - sion here, lost souls to seek.
our faith re - new, Glad - ly and joy - ful - ly Thy will to do.

3

2   Acquaint Thyself with Jesus.

Rev. J. B. Atchinson.

Geo. C. Stebbins.

1. Ac - quaint thy - self with Je - sus, The sin - ner's tru - est Friend;
2. Ac - quaint thy - self with Je - sus, No one like Him could lead;
3. Ac - quaint thy - self with Je - sus, And like Him thou shalt be;

A priv - i - lege most bless-ed To all He doth ex - tend.
No oth - er friend can help you In ev - ery time of need.
Transformed in - to His im - age, For all e - ter - ni - ty.

His love for man sur - pass - es The warm - est, earth-ly love;
No oth - er feels so deep - ly For all thy care and grief;
Ac - cept His of - fered mer - cy, Come, now, His prom-ise claim;

Ac - quaint thy - self with Je - sus, And His true friendship prove.
Ac - quaint thy - self with Je - sus, And He will give re - lief.
Ac - quaint thy - self with Je - sus, And spread a - broad His fame.

1

3   Christ Our Leader.

Rev. Robert F. Gordon.   Ira D. Sankey.

1. For Christ our Prince and Sav - iour, For truth and ho - li - ness,
2. The war we wage is blood-less, We fight not to de - stroy.
3. But Christ hath all the hon - or, 'Tis He that makes us strong,

We wage a con - stant war - fare, And on - ward bold - ly press;
The mot - to on our ban - ner, Is "Par - don, Peace, and Joy;"
The troph - ies of each con - quest, To Him a - lone be - long;

We brave the stern-est con - flict, By conscious strength in - spired,
We strive to free the cap - tive, Now held by sin a slave,
And His shall be the tri - umph, The glo - ry and re - nown,

Our hearts by fear un - shak - en, Our souls by cour - age fired.
To cheer the faint and hope-less, And make the trembling brave.
And His the praise ex - ult - ing, And His the vic - tor's crown.

5

4. The King is Here.

ALFRED J. HOUGH.

CHAS. H. GABRIEL.

1. As - sem-bled in the Mas-ter's name, Dis - ci-ples, here we meet to claim
2. His prom-ise is   to   ev -'ry one; Ask what ye will, it shall be done;
3. Such wealth of love His presence brings, The bread of life, the liv-ing springs;
4. His pres-ence shall our songs in-spire, His spir -it touch our lips with fire;

Ful - fil-ment of the prom-ise sweet, That Je-sus with His own will meet.
And   at His bless-ed feet we bow, For He is here to an-swer now.
All want we find in Him sup-plied, And we may all be sat-is-fied.
And bring the heav'nly life •so near, That all shall own the King is here.

Chorus.

The King is here! His Spir - it fills Our wait-ing hearts, con-trols our wills;

rit. ad lib.

His love dis-pels all doubt and fear; The King is here, the King is here!

Words of Cheer.

ALLEN A. JUDSON.   IRA D. SANKEY.

1. We come to-day from near and far, The light of hope our guid-ing star;
2. 'Tis good to meet in His dear name, And all His wondrous love proclaim;
3. O Sav-iour, bless our Christian band, For Thee en-list - ed, heart and hand;
4. And when we leave this hallowed place, O grant to us Thy heavenly grace;

In Je - sus' name we gath - er here, For strength and words of cheer.
To learn the way of life more clear, And hear glad words of cheer.
In - cline to us Thy gra-cious ear, And give us words of cheer.
In all our way, O be Thou near, To speak glad words of cheer.

Chorus.

O wondrous words, sweet words of cheer, That Je - sus speaks in tones so clear:

Still may they grow to us more dear, While gath-ered in His name.

6

Blessed Bible.

JULIA STERLING.   ROBERT D. GORDON.

1. Bless-ed Bi - ble, how we prize thee, God's own Word of life and love;
2. Bless-ed Bi - ble, gra-cious teach-er, Light that all the world may see;
3. Bless-ed Bi - ble, go thou with us Till we reach the last dark wave,

Bring-ing hope and joy and com - fort, Down to earth from heav'n a - bove.
We would read thy pre-cious pa - ges, And for coun - sel turn to thee.
Ev - er tell-ing of His mer - cy, Who a - lone is strong to save.

Had we not thy Law to guide us, And re - claim the wan-d'ring heart;
Thou the best, the pur-est treas-ure We could ask, or God be - stow,
Go thou with us till we en - ter Thro' the gates, the Cit - y fair;

We should sail o'er storm-y wa - ters, Like a ship with-out a chart.
May it be our high-est pleas-ure More and more of thee to know.
Till we see thy great In - spir - er, And a - dore His good-ness there.

8

7

More Like Thee.

F. J. Crosby

J. H. Burke.

1. Thou in whom no dark-ness dwelleth, Fill our souls with light di - vine;
2. Thou whose eye our hearts be-hold-eth, Search and prove us day by day;
3. To the work for each ap-point-ed, Ev - 'ry mo-ment may we give;

More and more in us re-flect - ed, May Thy pure ex - am - ple shine.
From the path that lead - eth up-ward, Suf - fer not our feet to stray.
Con - se-crat-ed to Thy serv-ice, For Thy glo - ry may we live.

Chorus.

O'er our words, our tho'ts and ac-tions, May we ev - er watch-ful be,

Grow-ing still, thro' grace and knowledge, More and more, O Lord, like Thee.

9

8   # A Foothold on the Rock.

Thos. MacKellar.

J. J. Lowe.

1. Give me a foothold on the Rock: The bil-lows round me roll:
2. Give me a foothold on the Rock, O Sav - iour of the lost!
3. Give me a foothold on the Rock, Till voic - es o'er the sea,

Let not their wild im - pet - uous shock O'er whelm my trembling soul;
The world and sin my strug-gles mock, And I am tem-pest-tossed.
Like even - ing chimings of the clock, Bid wel-come home to me.

O Thou that walk-est on the wave Thou Ru - ler of the sea
I strive to reach an anch'ring place; My Lord be Thou my stay;
The day of toil and watch-ing o'er, The night of sor-row past,

Stretch forth Thy might-y arm to save The soul that calls on Thee.
Ex - tend to me Thy hand of grace, Lest I be cast a - way.
I step up - on the shin-ing shore, And rest in peace at last.

10

9   All for Jesus

MARY D. JAMES.

GEO. C. STEBBINS.

✻ Duet.

1. All for Je - sus! all for Je - sus! All my be-ing's ransomed powers;
2. Let my hands perform His bidding; Let my feet run in His ways;
3. Since my eyes were fixed on Je-sus, I've lost sight of all be - side,—

All my thoughts and words and do-ings, All my days and all my hours.
Let my eyes see Je - sus on - ly; Let my lips speak forth His praise.
So enchained my spir-it's vis - ion, Looking at the Cru-ci - fied!

Quartet, or Chorus.

All for Je-sus! all for Je - sus! All my be-ing's ransomed pow'rs;
All for Je-sus! all for Je - sus! Let my feet run in His ways;
All for Je-sus! all for Je - sus! I've lost sight of all be-side;

All for Je - sus! all for Je - sus! All my days and all my hours.
All for Je - sus! all for Je - sus! Let my lips speak forth His praise.
All for Je-sus! all for Je - sus! All for Je - sus Cru-ci - fied!

✻ Sop & Ten., (or Alto Duet.) Alto singing Tenor part.

Copyright, 1894, by The Biglow & Main Co.

Bright Glory Land!

IDA G. TREMAINE.

HUBERT P. MAIN.

1. There is a land be-yond the stars, Glo-ry Land, bright Glo-ry Land!
2. The cit-y of our God is there, Glo-ry Land, bright Glo-ry Land!
3. We lift our eyes, by faith, and see, Glo-ry Land, bright Glo-ry Land!

Be-yond the sun-set's crim-son bars,— Glo-ry Land, bright Glo-ry Land!
Its jas-per walls with beau-ty fair, Glo-ry Land, bright Glo-ry Land!
Where Christ Him-self the light shall be, Glo-ry Land, bright Glo-ry Land!

A land of peace with-out al-loy; Of joy be-yond all earth-ly joy;
Its gates of pearl like sil-ver gleam, Its skies with fade-less sun light beam,
There songs of praise glad hearts shall sing; The ra-diant air with mu-sic ring;

And naught its calm can e'er de-stroy,—Glo-ry Land, bright Glo-ry Land!
And thro' it rolls life's crys-tal stream, Glo-ry Land, bright Glo-ry Land!
Each voice pro-claim our Sav-iour, King, Glo-ry Land, bright Glo-ry Land!

11 All for Christ.

LAURA E. NEWELL.   W. A. OGDEN.

1. We are workers in the Master's vineyard, "All for Christ, and Christ for all!"
2. Earn - est ev-er, and with true En-deav-or, We,will bear our cross each day;
3. Strong in faith, for Him we'll go and labor; Neath a bright, or frowning sky;

We will follow where the Saviour leads us, Gladly an - swer to His call.
Nought on earth our love for Him can sever, While we work and watch and pray.
Till we gather in His king-dom yon-der, With the faithful by and by.

Chorus.

Workers in His vine - yard, Faith-ful would we prove;
Work - ers in the Mas - ter's vine - yard, would we prove;

Ev - er loy-al, ev - er read - - y;— Strong in Je - sus' love!
ev - er read - y;—

13

12 Praise the Lord.

F. J. CROSBY.

H. P. DANKS.

1. Praise the Lord, let all with-in us Praise His name with sweet ac-cord;
2. If with all our hearts we seek Him, We shall find Him at the door;
3. Praise the Lord, ye ho-ly an-gels, Who ful-fil His high command;

For the com-fort of His Spir-it, And the teach-ing of His word.
He will par-don our transgressions, And re-mem-ber them no more.
Praise Him all ye saints in heav-en, While a-round His throne ye stand.

Chorus.

Praise the Lord, and give Him glo-ry For the work His grace has done;

From de-struc-tion He re-deems us, Thro' the blood of Christ the Son.

Copyright, 1894, by The Biglow & Main Co.

14

13   Forgetting Self in Thee.

GRACE J. FRANCES.   HUBERT P. MAIN.

1. We come to ask Thy bless-ing, Lord, And wor-ship at Thy feet;
2. We come to ask Thy bless-ing, Lord, That we may faith-ful prove,
3. We know not how to ask a-right, O help us, Lord, we pray;

O may The Spir-it now de-scend, While in Thy name we meet;
And from Thy word and Spir-it learn To trust, o-bey and love;
Up-hold us by Thy heav'nly grace, And ev-er guard our way;

O grant that thro' His pow'r di-vine, Each heart in-spir'd may be
From pride of heart and vain de-sire, O cleanse and make us free,
Do Thou di-rect our go-ing forth, Our Lead-er ev-er be;

To fol-low af-ter right-eous-ness, For-get-ting self in Thee.
That we henceforth Thy work may do, For-get-ting self in Thee.
Then shall we gain the vic-tor's crown, For-get-ting self in Thee.

14   He has Taken my Sins Away.

LYMAN G. CUYLER.

IRA D. SANKEY.

1. I will praise the Lord with heart and voice, And in Him I will re-joice;
2. When I came, with all my sin op-press'd, Un - to Him for peace and rest;
3. I will praise Him with my lat-est breath, For the vic - t'ry o - ver death;

I will sing His wondrous love to me, And this my song shall be,—
Then He heard my pray'r and set me free, And this my song shall be,—
I will praise Him thro' e - ter - ni - ty, And this my song shall be,—

Chorus.

He hath tak - - en my sins a - way, a - way, Praise His

He hath tak - en my sins a - way, ...

a - way,

ho - ly name, praise His ho - ly name; He hath tak - - en my

He hath tak - en m'

He has Taken my Sins Away.—Concluded

sins a - way, a - way, Hal - le - lu - jah to His name.
sins a - way,..........
a - way,

15   Light of the Wandering.

F. J. CROSBY.   Rev. ROBERT LOWRY.

1. Light of the wan - der - ing, Strength of the weak, Je - sus, Thou
2. Come to the des - o - late, Sad and op - press'd; Come to the
3. Come in our wea - ri - ness, Help us to pray; Lord, we would

Chorus.

Lamb of God, Thee would we seek.)
bro - ken heart Sigh - ing for rest. } Ten - der and pit - i - ful,
fol - low Thee; Show us the way.)

Lov - ing and mer - ci - ful, Je - sus, we plead with Thee; Hear Thou our cry.

16 I Am Coming.

M. R., arr.

IRA D. SANKEY.

1. I am com-ing, O my Sav-iour, For my heart is sad and sore;
2. I am com-ing, blest Redeem-er, I have heard Thy lov-ing call;
3. I am com-ing, Je-sus, Mas-ter, Guide my falt'ring steps a - right,
4. I am com-ing, though the tempter Bids my trem-bling soul de - spair,

And I seek the rest Thou giv - est Mine to be for ev - er - more.
And though sins un - told op-press me, Thou can'st save me from them all.
May the Ho - ly Spir - it lead me Out of dark - ness in - to light.
If I reach the door of mer - cy I shall nev - er per - ish there.

Chorus.

I am com-ing, I am com-ing, In my weak-ness, Lord, to Thee.

For I know Thou wilt re-ceive me, Thy sure prom-ise is my plea.

Copyright, 1894, by The Biglow & Main Co. 18

17   We Bless Thy Name, O Lord.

GRACE J. FRANCES.   HUBERT P. MAIN.

1. We bless Thy name, O Lord, While in Thy house we meet,
2. Thro' all our fleet-ing years, Thy word has been our stay,
3. Do Thou our love in-spire; And still our faith in-crease;
4. In all our com-ing days, O still our ref-uge be,

To lift our grate-ful hearts to Thee, And wor-ship at Thy feet.
It brought us safe with-in the fold, When we were far a-way.
Con-firm our hopes and keep us, Lord, In bonds of per-fect peace.
And may we all in sim-ple faith, Cling clos-er un-to Thee.

Refrain.

We bless Thy name, O Lord, For Thy pro-tect-ing care,

That gives to us with joy a-gain, This hallowed hour of prayer.

18 Gather the Golden Grain.

F. J. CROSBY.

IRA D. SANKEY.

1. Leave not for to-mor-row the work of to-day, For time, like an
2. Leave not for to-mor-row the work of to-day, The mo-ments are
3. Leave not for to-mor-row the work of to-day, The sum-mer is

ar - row, is speed-ing a - way; The har - vest is read-y, look
pre-cious, then why should we stay? The Mas-ter is call-ing a-
wan-ing, no lon-ger de-lay; The sheaves for the reap-ing wave

out on the plain; Go, thrust in the sick-le and gath-er the grain.
gain and a-gain; Go, thrust in the sick-le and gath-er the grain.
bright o'er the plain; Go, thrust in the sick-le and gath-er the grain.

Chorus.

Go, gath - er   Go, gath - er

Go, gath-er the gold-en grain;   Go, gath-er the gold-en grain; The

Gather the Golden Grain.—Concluded.

har-vest is read-y, look out on the plain; Go, gath-er the gold-en grain.

19   Shut in with Thee.

GRACE J. FRANCES.   HUBERT P. MAIN.

Prayerfully.

1. O Sav-iour, teach us how to pray And choose the words that we should speak;
2. Thou knowest, Lord, how frail we are, How prone to wan-der from Thy side;
3. E - ter - nal Spir-it, Ho - ly Dove, To seal our hearts the pow'r is Thine;

While gath-er'd here at close of day, Thy throne of grace to hum-bly seek.
O   keep us safe with-in Thy care, Be Thou our Shield, our Friend and Guide.
U - nite us in the bonds of love, And keep us one, thro' grace di - vine.

Chorus.   *rit. - - - - -*

Shut out the world, and let us be For one sweet hour shut in with Thee.

21

Overcoming in His Name.

JENNIE WILSON.

W. A. OGDEN.

1. In the ho - ly Christian war - fare, We the help of Christ may claim;
2. Tho' the foes we meet be ma - ny, Sure - ly we have naught to fear,
3. Let us nev - er grow faint-heart-ed, Or in weakness yield to strife;
4. To each soul that o - ver - com - eth, Heaven's fade-less palms be-long;

And thro' grace di - vine may con-quer, O - ver - com-ing in His name.
Trust-ing in the "Friend of sin - ners," Who is ev - er, ev - er near,
But be loy - al to our Lead - er, And ob - tain the crown of life.
When be-yond all sounds of con - flict, Swells the victor's glad new song.

Refrain.

O - ver-com-ing in His name,..... O - ver-com-ing in His name;

His name,

Praise the Lord! we shall be vic - tors, O - ver - com - ing in His name.

21   Come In, O Lord!

RIAN A. DYKES.

IRA D. SANKEY.

1. Thy voice, O Lord, I've heard once more, O help me now un-bar the door;
2. I've heard Thy gen-tle knock be-fore, But would not give my i-dols o'er;
3. O bless-ed Friend no lon-ger stand, With ach-ing brow, and pierced hand

And bid Thee wel-come to my heart, Nor cause Thee ev-er to de-part.
O hear my ear-nest pray'r to-day, I can-not let Thee go a-way.
Out-side the door, 'tis o-pen wide; Come in, and ev-er-more a-bide.

Chorus.

Come in,...... Come in,......

Come in, O Lord, come in; Come in, O Lord, come in;

And cleanse this sin-ful heart of mine, Come in, O Lord, come in!

22   Jesus, I am Resting.

JEAN S. PIGOTT, by per.   R. DONALD JONES.

1. Je - sus! I am rest - ing, rest-ing   In   the joy of what Thou art;
2. Oh, how great Thy lov - ing kind-ness, Vast-er, broad-er than the   sea!
3. Sim - ply trust-ing Thee, Lord Je - sus,   I   be-hold Thee as Thou art,
4. Ev - er lift Thy face up-on me,   As   I watch and wait for Thee;

I   am find - ing out   the great-ness Of   Thy lov - ing heart.
Oh, how mar - vel - ous Thy good-ness, Lav-ished all   on   me!
And Thy love so pure, so change-less, Sat - is - fies   my heart;
Rest - ing 'neath Thy smile, Lord Je - sus, Earth's dark shad-ows flee.

Thou hast bid me gaze up-on Thee, And Thy beau-ty fills my   soul,
Yes, I rest in Thee, Be-lov - ed, Know what wealth of grace is Thine,
Sat - is - fies its deep - est long-ings, Meets, and fills its   ev - ery need,
Bright-ness of my Fa-ther's glo - ry, Sun - shine of my Fa-ther's face,

For,   by Thy trans - form - ing pow - er, Thou hast made me whole.
Know Thy cer - tain - ty   of prom ise, And have made it   mine.
Crowns my life with dai - ly bless-ings: Thine is love in - deed!
Keep me ev - er trust - ing, rest - ing, Fill   me with Thy grace.

24

23 The Home-land Shore.

F. J. CROSBY.   S. C. FOSTER, arr.

1. Far, far be-yond the storms that gath-er Dark o'er our way,
2. Far, far be-yond the roll-ing bil-lows, Faith spreads her wings;
3. Far, far be-yond the vale and shadow, Loved ones have passed;
4. O bless-ed morn of joy un-bounded, O glo-rious day;

There shines the light of joy e-ter-nal, Bright in the realms of day.
Love tells us of the gold-en Cit-y, Hope, of its glo-ry sings.
We'll meet them in the "ma-ny mansions," All gathered home at last.
There ev-ery tear of grief and an-guish Je-sus shall wipe a-way.

Chorus.

There shall sor-row, pain and part-ing, Grieve our hearts no more;

Soon, soon we'll meet be-yond the riv-er, Safe on the Home-land shore.

24   On Thee My Heart is Resting!

Rev. Theod. Monod.

B. C. Unseld.

1. On Thee my heart is rest-ing! Ah, this is rest in-deed!
2. My guilt is great, but great-er The mer-cy Thou dost give;
3. When clouds are dark-est round me, Thou, Lord, art then most near,

What else, al-might-y Sav-iour, Can a poor sin-ner need?
Thy-self, a spot-less Of-f'ring, Hast died that I should live.
My droop-ing faith to quick-en, My wea-ry soul to cheer.

Thy light is all my wis-dom, Thy love is all my stay;
With Thee, my soul un-fet-tered Has ris-en from the dust;
Safe rest-ing on Thy bo-som, I gaze up-on Thy face;

Our Fa-ther's home in glo-ry Draws near-er ev-'ry day.
Thy blood is all my treas-ure, Thy word is all my trust.
In vain my foes would drive me From Thee, my hid-ing-place.

On Thee My Heart is Resting!—Concluded.

Chorus.

On Thee my heart is rest-ing! Ah, this is rest in-deed!

What else, al-might-y Sav-iour, Can a poor sin-ner need?

4 'Tis Thou hast made me happy,
  'Tis Thou hast set me free,
  To whom shall I give glory
  For ever, but to Thee?

Of earthly love and blessing
  Should every stream run dry,
  Thy grace shall still be with me,
  Thy grace, to live and die!—*Cho.*

25   Precious, Happy Meeting.

GRACE J. FRANCES.   HUBERT P. MAIN.

1. Pre-cious, hap-py meet-ing, Joy-ful hour of prayer;
2. Thou hast brought us hith-er By Thy gra-cious hand;
3. In the bonds of friend-ship, May we still re-main;

Sav-iour, we a-dore Thee, For Thy watch-ful care.
Grant us now Thy Spir-it, Bless our youth-ful band.
Sav-iour, be Thou with us Till we meet a-gain.

27

26   Do Something for Jesus To-day!

J. NICHOLSON.

IRA D. SANKEY.

1. Do some-thing for Je-sus to - day! Re-mem-ber what He did for you!
2. Do some-thing for Je-sus to - day! Bring some one to bow at His feet!
3. Do some-thing for Je-sus to - day! The moments, how swiftly they roll!
4. Do some-thing for Je-sus to - day! Go speak to the per-ish-ing one

Let ev - ery En-deav'rer now say, "Lord, what wilt Thou have me to do?"
For He is the "Life and the Way,"—All work for the Mas - ter is sweet.
Now res - cue the lost ones who say, That "no man doth care for my soul."
Whom Sa-tan hath led far a - stray: To-mor-row he may be un - done!

Refrain.

Do some - - thing to - day,...... No lon - - ger

Do some-thing to - day, to-day,   No lon-ger de - lay;

O hast - en a - way, no lon - ger de-lay, Do some-thing for Je-sus to - day!

27   Precious Saviour.

L. M. ROUSE, arr.   DORA BOOLE.

1. Pre-cious Sav-iour, I will praise Thee, Thine, and on-ly Thine I am;
2. Long my yearn-ing heart was try-ing To en-joy this per-fect rest;
3. I am trust-ing ev-ery mo-ment, In the precious blood ap-plied;
4. Con-se-crat-ed to Thy ser-vice, I would live and die for Thee,

For the cleans-ing blood has reached me; Glo-ry, glo-ry to the Lamb.
But when I gave o-ver "*trying*,"—Simply trust-ing, I was blest.
Calm-ly rest-ing at the fount-ain, Dwelling at my Saviour's side.
Glad-ly tell the wondrous sto-ry Of sal-va-tion full and free.

Chorus.

Glo-ry, glo-ry, Je-sus saves me, Bless-ed be His ho-ly name;

For the cleansing blood has reached me, Hal-le-lu-jah to the Lamb.

28   Anywhere, My Saviour.

E. C. ELLSWORTH.

J. H. TENNEY.

1. A - ny-where, my Sav - iour, lead my will - ing feet, On - ly let me
2. A - ny-where, my Sav - iour, on - ly on me smile, Strengthen, guard, and
3. A - ny-where, my Sav - iour, on - ly this I pray, Keep me in the

clasp Thy hand, feel Thy pres-ence sweet; Thorns may pierce and snares beset,
com - fort me, let not sin be - guile; Dark and toil-some tho' my way,
nar - row path, nev - er let me stray; Sin may plead with sy - ren voice,

I will fol - low Thee, A - ny-where, my Sav-iour, if Thou lead-est me.
I will nev - er fear, A ny-where, my Sav-iour, if Thy pres-ence cheer.
Help me answer nay, Kept by Thee, my Sav-iour, I will hold my way.

Chorus.

A - - - ny-where, my bless - ed Sav - iour,

A - ny-where with Thee,   If Thou on - ly lead - est me

Anywhere, My Saviour.—Concluded.

A . . . ny -

I will fol-low Thee, I will fol-low Thee, A-ny-where with Thee,

where, my bless - ed Sav - iour, If Thou lead-est me.........

I will ev - er fol-low Thee, If Thou lead-est me (lead-est me).

29   Sweet the Moments.

JAMES ALLEN.   Sicilian Melody.

1. Sweet the mo-ments, rich in bless-ing, Which be-fore the cross we spend ;
2. Tru - ly bless-ed is this sta - tion, Low be-fore His cross to lie,
3. Love and grief our hearts di - vid - ing, With our tears His feet we bathe;
4. For Thy sor - rows we a-dore Thee, For the pains that wrought our peace,

Life, and health, and peace pos-sess-ing, From the sin-ner's dy-ing Friend.
While we see di - vine com-pas-sion, Beam-ing in His gra-cious eye.
Con-stant still, in faith a - bid - ing, Life de - riv-ing from His death.
Gra-cious Sav-iour! we im-plore Thee In our souls Thy love in-crease.

30 Because He Loves Me so.

E. H. Miller.   Rian A. Dykes.

Moderato.

1. I love to hear the sto - ry Which an - gel - voic - es tell,
2. I'm glad my bless - ed Sav - iour Was once a child like me,
3. To sing His love and mer - cy, My sweet - est songs I'll raise;

How once the King of glo - ry Came down on earth to dwell;
To show how pure and ho - ly His lit - tle ones might be;
And tho' I can - not see Him, I know He hears my praise;

I am both weak and sin - ful, But this I sure - ly know, ..
And if I try to fol - low His foot-steps here be - low, ...
For He has kind - ly promised That e - ven I may go......

The Lord came down to save me, Be - cause He loved me so.
He nev - er will for - get me, Be - cause He loves me so.
To sing a - mong His an - gels, Be - cause He loves me so.

31   Praise His Name forever.

F. J. CROSBY.   IRA D. SANKEY.

1. The Lord is ev - er gra-cious, To those who do His will;
2. He sends His ben - e - dic-tions With each re - turn - ing day;
3. Our cup is filled with bless-ings, And o - ver-flows with love;

His good-ness and His mer - cy Their steps will fol - low still.
He gives us joy and glad-ness, And takes our sins a - way.
He draws us by His spir - it To yon bright home a - bove.

Chorus.

Then praise His name for - ev - er, His wondrous love pro - claim;

Let all the peo - ple praise Him, And mag - ni - fy His name.

33

32   Anywhere with Jesus.

ROBERT SHAW.

J. E. EDWARDS.

1. A - ny-where with Je - sus, glad - ly would I go; At His side there's
2. A - ny-where with Je - sus, this my song to - day, Mas-ter, I will
3. A - ny-where with Je - sus, He will be my guide, In His own pa -

safe - ty from the cru - el foe; A - ny-where with Je - sus,
fol - low, fol - low all the way; A - ny-where with Je - sus,
vil - ion I can safe - ly hide; A - ny-where with Je - sus,

this my pray'r shall be, Help me, O my Sav-iour, still to fol-low Thee.
in the dark-est hour, He will ev - er keep me by His might-y pow'r.
this is all I need; In His love a - bid-ing, this is rest in - deed.

Refrain. (*May be repeated softly.*)

A - ny-where, a - ny-where, thro' this world be - low,

Copyright, 1893, by The Biglow & Main Co.

34

Anywhere with Jesus.—Concluded.

With my Sav - iour lead - ing, glad - ly would I go.

33 Saviour, Breathe an Evening Blessing.

JAMES EDMESTON.   D. BORTNIANSKI.

1. { Sav-iour, breathe an evening bless-ing, Ere re - pose our spir - its seal;
   { Sin and want we come con-fess - ing; Thou canst save and Thou canst heal. }

2. { Tho' the night be dark and drear - y, Dark-ness can-not hide from Thee;
   { Thou art He who, nev - er wea - ry, Watcheth where Thy peo-ple be. }

Though de - struc-tion walk a - round us, Tho' the ar - row near us fly,
Should swift death this night o'er-take us, And our couch be - come our tomb,

An - gel guards from Thee surround us, We are safe if Thou art nigh.
May the morn in Heav'n a - wake us, Clad in light and death-less bloom.

34 Praise ye the Lord.

GRACE J. FRANCES.

HUBERT P. MAIN.

1. Praise ye the Lord, the Rock of our sal - va - tion; Praise ye His
2. Praise ye the Lord, and in His tem - ple kneel - ing; Pour out your
3. Praise ye the Lord, and may your faith as - cend - ing; Turn from the

name and come be - fore His throne; Tell of His love with
hearts in ferv - ent, grate - ful prayer; List to His voice in
world to pur - er joys a - bove; O may His grace from

ho - ly ad - o - ra - tion Praise the Lord, for He is God a - lone.
ten - der ac-cents steal - ing, Cast on Him your ev-ery weight of care.
ev - ery snare de - fend - ing, Keep your hearts in per-fect peace and love.

Chorus.

Praise ye the Lord, whose truth a - bid - eth ev - er, Glo - rious and

Praise ye the Lord.—Concluded.

great are all His works and ways, Praise ye the Lord, let

all the peo-ple praise Him, Praise the Lord, whose mer-cy crowns your days.

35   Come, Holy Ghost.

ASAHEL NETTLETON.   (MEAR. C. M.)   American, 1740.

1. Come, Ho - ly Ghost, my soul in - spire; This one great gift im - part—
2. Bear wit - ness I am born a - gain, My ma - ny sins for-given:
3. More of my - self grant I may know, From sin's de - ceit be free;

What most I need, and most de - sire, An hum - ble, ho - ly heart.
Nor let a gloom - y doubt re - main To cloud my hope of heav'n.
In all the Chris-tian grac - es grow, And live a - lone to Thee.

37

36

Thine, O Lord.

W. MAXWELL, arr.   J. H. BURKE.

1. Thine, O Lord, and Thine for - ev - er; Pur:has'd with Thy pre-cious blood:
2. Thine, O Lord, and Thine for - ev - er; Res-cued from the ty-rant's thrall;
3. Thine, O Lord, and Thine for - ev - er; Thine to fol-low, serve, a - dore;

Bonds of love that nought can sev - er, Bind my soul to Thee, my God.
Thou wilt keep who didst de - liv - er— Make me vic - tor o - ver all.
O may this be my en-deav-or Still to praise Thee more and more.

Chorus.

Thine, O Lord,.......... to - day and ev - - er;
Lord, to - day and ev - er, Thine, O Lord, to - day and ev - er;

Thine to com - - - fort, keep, and guide,..........
com - fort, keep, and guide, Thine to com fort, keep, and guide,

Copyright, 1894, by The Biglow & Main Co.

Thine, O Lord.—Concluded.

Till be - yond.......... the roll-ing riv - - er

be - yond the roll - ing riv - er, Till be - yond the roll - ing riv - er

I be - hold.............. Thee glo - ri - fied............

be - hold Thee, I be - hold ... glo - ri - fied.

37   Great Shepherd of the Sheep.

AMOS R. WELLS.   (BOYLSTON. S. M.)   LOWELL MASON.

1. Great Shep-herd of the sheep, In Thy one fold of love
2. Seek we each oth - er's weal, Share we each oth - er's woe,
3. Near - er, O Lord, to Thee; Near - er our broth - er then;

Thy ma - ny chil - dren guard and keep Like that great throng a - bove.
Low at one com - mon al - tar kneel, One com-mon pur - pose know.
Till the wide world, from sea to sea, Join in one glad A - men.

38 The Chief among Ten Thousand.

F. J. CROSBY.

GEO. C. STEBBINS.

1. "He's the Chief a - mong ten thousand," My Re-deem-er and my King!
2. When my earth-ly course is fin-ished, And the work of life is done,
3. I shall see Him in His beau-ty, And His hand will wipe a - way

I shall wor-ship and a - dore Him, And His praise for - ev - er sing.
When the bat-tle-cry is o - ver, And the vic-tor's crown is won;
Ev - 'ry tear of pain and sor-row, While His gen-tle voice will say,

"He's the Lil - y of the val - ley," And the fair - est of the fair!
I shall cast my crown be-fore Him, I shall walk with Him in white,
"Come, ye bless-ed of my Fa - ther, To the rest prepared a - bove,"

I shall see Him in His glo - ry, Where the ma - ny man-sions are.
Where the sil - ver fount-ains spar-kle, 'Mid the vales of end - less light.
Where the tree of life is bloom-ing, In my home of peace and love.

The Chief among Ten Thousand.—Concluded.

Chorus.

"He's the Chief a-mong ten thousand," And the fair-est of the fair;

I shall see Him in His beau-ty, And His im-age I shall bear.

39   Reception Hymn.

AMOS R. WELLS.   HUBERT P. MAIN.

1. Glad-ly the serv-ants of the King En-large their work-ing band, ...
2. Blest is his work who toils a - lone To serve the bless-ed Lord; ...
3. Their coun-sels wise are man - i - fold, A hun-dred arms to stay, ...
4. Teach us to work to-geth-er here, And bless our broth-er - hood; ...

Re - joice with songs of wel-com-ing To seize a broth-er's hand. ...
But my-riad joys the ma-ny own Who work with one ac - cord. ....
A hun-dred hands that will up-hold Up-on a doubt-ful way. ....
What Thou dost hate, our on - ly fear, Thy joy our on - ly good. ...

40   The Mansions of Light.

JOHN H. YATES.   IRA D. SANKEY.

1. O the man-sions of light, bliss-ful man-sions of light, We are
2. There no night spreads its man-tle o'er val - leys and hills, Hid - ing
3. Yet a lit - tle while here for the wings of the years Speed us

com-ing their glo - ry   to   see; We are com-ing thro' temp-est, thro'
beau-ties and glo-ries un - told; There no win-ter shall si - lence the
on   to that far - a - way shore—Then a - way we shall fly from this

sor - row and night, With the King in   His beau - ty to   be.
song of   the rills, And the dwell-ers shall nev - er grow old.
val - ley of tears To the land where they sor - row no more.

Chorus.

For   we know if this house we in - hab - it to - day Were dis-

The Mansions of Light.—Concluded.

solved in the depths of the tomb, We've a build-ing of God, in that

land far a - way, Where the Spring-time for ev - er shall bloom.

41   Holy Ghost, with Light Divine.

ANDREW REED.   L. M. GOTTSCHALK, arr. by H. P. M.

1. Ho - ly Ghost, with light di - vine, Shine up - on this heart of mine;
2. Ho - ly Ghost, with pow'r di - vine, Cleanse this guilt - y heart of mine;
3. Ho - ly Ghost, with joy di - vine, Cheer this saddened heart of mine;
4. Ho - ly Spir - it, all di - vine, Dwell with - in this heart of mine;

Chase the shades of night a - way, Turn my dark-ness in - to day.
Long hath sin, with-out con - trol, Held do - min - ion o'er my soul.
Bid my ma - ny woes de - part, Heal my wound-ed, bleed-ing heart.
Cast down ev - ery i - dol-throne, Reign su-preme—and reign a - lone.

42   The Lion of Judah.

HENRY Q. WILSON, arr .

HENRY TUCKER, arr.

1. 'Twas Je - sus, my Sav-iour, who died on the tree, To o - pen a
2. And when I was will-ing with all things to part, He gave me His
3. Tho' round me the storms of ad-ver-si - ty roll, And the waves of de-
4. And when with the ransomed, by Je - sus my head, From fount-ain to

fount - ain for sin - ners like me; His blood is that foun-tain which
bless - ing, His love in my heart, So now I am joined with the
struc - tion en - com - pass my soul; In vain this frail ves - sel the
fount - ain I then shall be led; I'll fall at His feet and His

par - don be - stows, And cleans - es the foul - est wher - ev - er it flows.
con - quer-ing band Who are marching to glo - ry at Je - sus' command.
tem-pest shall toss—My hope is se-cure thro' the blood of the cross.
mer - cy a - dore, And sing Hal-le - lu - jah to God ev - er-more.

Chorus.

For the Li - on of Ju - dah shall break ev - ery chain,

44

The Lion of Judah.—Concluded.

And gave us the vic - t'ry a - gain and a - gain.

43　　　　　　　**All My Journey.**

F J. Crosby.

H. P. Danks.

1. Lov-ing Sav-iour, gra-cious Lord, Ev - er trust-ing in Thy word,
2. In my weak-ness,Thou art strong; In my sad-ness Thou my song,
3. All my foot-steps Thou wilt guide, Till I reach the swell-ing tide;

Day by day I'll fol-low Thee, Tho' my way I can-not see;
Tho' the bil - lows o'er me roll, Thou, the ref - uge of my soul:
Then up - on Thy lov - ing breast, Thou wilt bear me home to rest:

'Tis e - nough that still I know, All my jour-ney Thou wilt go.
O how sweet that still I know, All my jour-ney Thou wilt go.
There, what joy 'twill be to know, Why my Sav-iour loved me so.

44 Scatter Sunshine.

LANTA W. SMITH.

E. O. EXCELL.

1. In a world where sor-row Ev - er will be known, Where are found the
2. Slightest ac - tions oft - en Meet the sor-est needs, For the world wants
3. When the days are gloom-y, Sing a hap - py song, Meet the world's re-

need - y, And the sad and lone; How much joy and comfort You can
dai - ly, Lit - tle kind - ly deeds; O, what care and sor-row, You may
pin - ing With a cour-age strong; Go with faith un-daunted, Thro' the

all be - stow, If you scat-ter sun-shine Ev-erywhere you go.
help re - move, With your songs of gladness, Sym-pa-thy and love.
ills of life, Scatter smiles and sunshine, O'er its toil and strife.

Chorus.

Scat - - - ter sun-shine all a - long your way, Cheer and bless and
Scat - ter smiles and

-16-

Scatter Sunshine.—Concluded.

bright-en Ev - cry pass-ing day. Ev - cry pass-ing day.

45   I Need Thee Every Hour.

ANNIE S. HAWKS.   Rev. ROBERT LOWRY.

1. I need Thee ev-'ry hour, Most gra-cious Lord; No ten-der voice like
2. I need Thee ev-'ry hour; Stay Thou near by; Temptations lose their
3. I need Thee ev-'ry hour, In joy or pain; Come quickly and a -
4. I need Thee ev-'ry hour; Teach me Thy will; And Thy rich promise-
5. I need Thee ev-'ry hour, Most Ho - ly one; O, make me Thine in-

Refrain.

Thine Can peace af - ford.
pow'r When Thou art nigh.
bide, Or life is vain.   I need Thee, O! I need Thee;
es In me ful - fil.
deed, Thou bless - ed Son.

Ev - 'ry hour I need Thee; O bless me now, my Saviour! I come to Thee.

Copyright, 1872, by R. Lowry. Used by per.   -17

46 I Steal away to Thee.

JULIA STERLING.   H. P. DANKS.

1. There is a place of ref - uge, More dear than all be - side,
2. With - in that vale of si - lence, Of calm and sweet re - pose,
3. No voice like Thine, so ten - der, Can soothe my ach - ing heart;

A vale of ho - ly si - lence, Where wea - ry souls may hide:
Where peace dis-pels all sad - ness, And like a riv - er flows;
No words like Thine, so pre - cious, Can bid my fears de - part:

And when the day is end - ed, And I from toil am free,
I hear a whispered mes - sage, That tells Thy love to me;
And when fall even - ing shad-ows, O wel - come hour to me!

O bless - ed, bless - ed Sav - iour, I steal a - way to Thee.
And then, by faith di - rect - ed, I steal a - way to Thee.
'Tis then for sweet com - mun - ion I steal a - way to Thee.

48

47 Fill Your Lamp.

GRACE J. FRANCES.   HUBERT P. MAIN.

1. Hast thou trimm'd thy lamp, my brother, Is it burn-ing clear and bright?
2. Is it shin - ing in the dark-ness Where the wea - ry wand'rers roam?
3. For the com - ing of the Bridegroom, And the mar-riage feast pre-pare;

Is it shin - ing so that oth - ers, May be - hold its steady light?
Will its rays, their steps il - lum - ing, Help to guide them safe-ly home?
Let thy lamp be trimm'd and burn-ing When He bids thee en - ter there.

Chorus.

O be watch-ful, ev - er watch-ful, For the Bridegroom draweth near;

And be sure thy lamp is burn-ing, When the summons thou shalt hear.

48   Go Tell the Glad Tidings.

ISAAC G. MITCHELL.   W. A. OGDEN.

1. Go tell the glad ti - dings of Je - sus, so sweet, Of Je - sus who
2. Go tell the glad ti - dings of Je - sus, so sweet, Till all, of His
3. Go tell the glad ti - dings of mer - cy and love, To lost ones wher-

came from a - bove; The mes-sage of mer - cy to sinners repeat, The
mer - cy shall know; And come with re - joic - ing to bow at His feet, Re -
e'er they may be; That souls may be won for the kingdom a-bove, And

sto - ry of in - fin - ite love.
deemed from their sorrow and woe.   }   Go tell the glad ti - dings a -
own their sal - va - tion to thee.

Chorus.

gain,.... And glad - ly sing out the re - frain;.... The mes-sage is
a - gain,   re-frain;

Go Tell the Glad Tidings.—Concluded.

true; what more can we do Than tell the old sto - ry a - gain?

49 Lord, I Bow at Thy Throne.

WM. STEVENSON.   Rev. ROBERT LOWRY.

1. Lord, I bow at Thy throne, My un - wor - thi - ness own, To Thy
2. If my sins I con - fess, Thou wilt heark-en and bless, For Thy
3. Lord, my guilt I la - ment, And in sor - row re - pent; Red like

cross and Thy promise I cling; O how bless-ed the tho't, Thou my
mer - cy is boundless and free; All Thy goodness may share, None need
crim - son my sins are, I know; Naught can save but Thy blood; Cleanse me

par - don hast bought, And no mon - ey or price need I bring.
ev - er de - spair, But re - joice Thy sal - va - tion to see.
now in that flood, And my soul shall be whit - er than snow.

51

50   Look Up, and Rejoice!

E. A. GIRVIN, arr.

CHAS. H. GABRIEL.

1. Look up, and re-joice! for the light is now shin-ing, Lift up ye the
2. Look up, and re-joice! for the light is now shin-ing, Look up, and the
3. Look up, and re-joice! for the light is now shin-ing, Look up, and a -

fall - en, and res - cue the lost; "For Christ and the Church," this your
glad - ness of heav - en re - ceive; Thy heart with the pres - ence of
way thro' the calm e - ther sky; Where Christ with His own soon in

con - stant En-deav - or, Be loy - al to Je - sus, what-ev - er the cost.
Je - sus o'er - flow-ing,—How sweet in the truth of His word to be-lieve.
tri - umph shall bring thee To beau - ti - ful mansions pre-par - ing on high.

Chorus.

Look up, look up, His ho - ly word be-lieve; Look up, look up, His

Look Up, and Rejoice!—Concluded.

bless-ing now re - ceive, "For Christ and the Church," this your con-stant En -

deav - or, Be loy - al to Je - sus, what-ev - er the cost.

51 Jesus shall Reign.

I. WATTS.   (DUKE STREET. L. M.)   JOHN HATTON.

1. Je - sus shall reign where'er the sun Does his suc-ces-sive jour-ney's run;
2. To Him shall end-less pray'r be made, And praises throng to crown His head:
3. Peo-ple and realms of ev - ery tongue Dwell on His love with sweetest song;
4. Blessings a-bound where'er He reigns, The prisoner leaps to loose his chains;

His kingdom stretch from shore to shore, Till moons shall wax and wane no more.
His name, like sweet perfume shall rise With ev-ery morn-ing sac - ri - fice.
And in-fant voi - ces shall pro-claim Their ear-ly bless-ings on His name.
The wea-ry find e - ter - nal rest, And all the sons of want are blest.

52. The Song of My Soul.

IDA SCOTT TAYLOR.   W. A. OGDEN.

1. There's a song in my soul that keeps ring-ing Its mel - o - dy
2. Oh this won - der - ful song how it thrills me, With rapt'rous and
3. And what - ev - er my earth - ly con - di - tion, To oth - ers this
4. When this life's wea - ry jour - ney is end - ed, And I, with Thy

all the day long, And ev - er my spir - it keeps sing-ing This
ho - ly de - light; Its sweet-ness pos - sess - es, and fills me, With
song I will give, And oh, it shall be my sweet mis - sion, To
glo - ri - fied throng, To yon - der bright courts have as-cend - ed, My

Chorus.

beau - ti - ful, beau - ti - ful song.
glad - ness, from morn - ing 'till night.
sing it as long as I live.
soul shall keep sing - ing this song.

O Sav - iour, Thou art the

theme (the theme), And dai - ly Thy love I'll ex - tol, Thou did'st

The Song of My Soul.—Concluded.

suf - fer my life to re - deem,.... And Thou art the song of my soul.
re - deem,

53   "It is Finished."

Rev. J. Proctor.
                       Ira D. Sankey.

1. Noth - ing ei - ther great or small—Nothing, sin - ner, no;   Je - sus died and
2. When He, from His loft - y throne, Stoop'd to do and   die;   Ev - 'ry thing was
3. Wea - ry, work-ing, burden'd one, Wherefore toil you so?   Cease your do-ing;
4. Cast your dead-ly "do-ing" down—Down at Je - sus' feet;   Stand in Him, in

Chorus.

paid it all, Long, long a - go.
ful - ly done: Hearken to His cry.
all was done Long, long a - go.
Him a - lone, Graciously com - plete.
} "It is fin-ish'd!" yes, in-deed,

Finished ev - ery jot; Sin-ner, this is all you need, Tell me, is it not?

Copyright, 1894, by The Biglow & Main Co.

55

Let us Labor and be Faithful.

GRACE J. FRANCES.   HUBERT P. MAIN.

1. Do not let us lon-ger tar-ry when there's work that must be done, And the
2. Let us haste with joy and gladness while the summer days are bright, And the
3. For, be-hold! the time is fly-ing, and the day will soon be o'er, Let us

Lord of the harvest calls today: There are sheaves that must be gather'd ere the
reapers now are singing on the plain; They are toil-ing late and ear-ly, but their
la-bor for the Master while we may; For the night is fast approaching when our

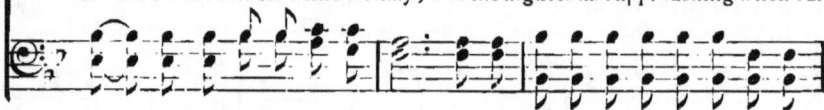

set-ting of the sun, And our moments, like the shadows, fly a-way.
will-ing hearts are light, While they gather in the sheaves of gold-en grain.
hands can work no more, O be read-y when He call-eth us a-way.

Refrain.

Let us la-bor and be faith-ful all the day (all the day;) Let us

Let us Labor.—Concluded.

la - bor and be ear-nest while we may (while we may); For the resting-time will

come, and our Lord will call us home, If we la-bor and are faithful while 'tis day.

55 The Lord's my Shepherd.

"Rouse's Version." 1643.   (AZMON. C. M.)   C. G. GLASER.

1. The Lord's my Shepherd, I'll not want, He makes me down to lie
2. My soul He doth re - store a - gain, And me to walk doth make,
3. Yea, though I walk in death's dark vale, Yet will I fear no ill;
4. Good-ness and mer - cy all my life Shall sure - ly fol - low me;

In pas-tures green; He lead-eth me   The qui - et wa - ters by.
With - in the paths of righteousnes,   Ev'n for His own name's sake.
For Thou art with me; and Thy rod   And staff me com - fort still.
And in God's house for - ev er - more My dwell-ing-place shall be.

56   O Christian, Speed Thee.

J. H. YATES.

IRA D. SANKEY.

1. O   Christian, speed thee on thy way, Lay ev - ery bur-den   down;
2. For - get the things which are behind—The sins and fol - lies past;
3. A   cloud of wit-ness - es   be-hold Thy pro-gress in the way;
4. On Je - sus fix thy longing eyes; The au - thor of thy faith

For thee the King doth now display, In realms of ev - er - last - ing day,
Increasing strength thy soul shall find; Then on-ward, on-ward like the wind,
Press on! thy tri-umph shall be told By an - gel choirs with harps of gold,
Shall help thee win the glorious prize, And bid thee welcome to the skies,

A   nev - er fad - ing   crown, A nev - er fad - ing   crown.
And to   the course hold fast, And to the course hold fast.
When comes the crown-ing day, When comes the crown-ing day.
When fall the shades of death, When fall the shades of death.

Chorus.

Then speed a-way! then speed a - way! Lay ev - ery bur - den down,

O Christian, Speed Thee.—Concluded.

O look not back, but on-ward press, And gain the promised crown.

57   My Heart is Resting.

ANNA L. WARING, by per.   JHAN A. DYKES.

1. My heart is rest-ing, O my God, I will give thanks and sing:
2. Now the frail ves-sel Thou hast made, No hand but Thine shall fill—
3. I thirst for springs of heav'nly life, And here all day they rise;

My heart is at the se-cret source Of ev-'ry pre-cious thing.
The wa-ters of the earth have failed, And I am thirst-y still.
I seek the treas-ure of Thy love, And close at hand it lies.

4 And a "new song" is in my mouth,
To long-loved music set—
Glory to Thee for all the grace
I have not tasted yet!

5 I have a heritage of joy
That yet I must not see;
The hand that bled to make it mine
Is keeping it for me,

58 Building for Eternity.

F. J. CROSBY.
Moderato.

H. P. DANKS.

1. We are build-ing day by day, While we on-ward press our
2. We are build-ing day by day, O di-rect us, Lord, we
3. We are build-ing day by day, In the lov-ing words we

way, And the thot's that fill the heart, Of our build-ing, form a part.
pray; If sup-port-ed by Thy hand, Sure-ly, then, our house shall stand.
say, In the deeds of kindness done, And the vic-t'ries we have won.

Chorus.

We are build-ing day by day, As we on-ward press our way;

Build-ing not for time are we,— Build-ing for e-ter-ni-ty.

59 Light of Life.

HORATIUS BONAR, D.D.

GEO. C. STEBBINS.

1. Light of Life, so soft-ly shin-ing From the cross of Cal-va-ry;
2. Light of Life, that knows no fad-ing, From all chang-es Thou art free;
3. Light of Life, that knows no set-ting, Day and night Thy beams we see;
4. Light of Life, in days of gladness, To Thy radience we would flee;

Nev-er wan-ing, nor de-clin-ing, Shine on me, O shine on me.
Ho-ly Light, that knows no shading, Shine on me, O shine on me.
Joy and peace in us be get-ting, Shine on me, O shine on me.
Be our strength in days of sad-ness, Shine on me, O shine on me.

Chorus.

Shine on me, O shine on me, Light of Life, O shine on me;

With the love of Je-sus beaming, Shine on me, O shine on me.

Send Out the Glad Tidings.

IDA C. LEWIS.

CHAS. H GABRIEL.

1. Send out the glad ti-dings, sal-va-tion is free; Re-demp-tion was
2. Send out the glad ti-dings, no lon-ger de-lay; For mill-ions are
3. Send out the glad ti-dings, the sto-ry re-peat From cel-lar and
4. Send out the glad ti-dings—O hast-en the day, When men of all

pur-chas'd on Cal-va-ry's tree For you and for me, and for
dy-ing, who know not the way; Who know not that Christ, the Re-
house-top, thro' al-ley and street: To those who have wan-dered far
na-tions shall Je-sus o-bey: When ban-ners tri-umph-ant are

all who be-lieve:"There's life for a look"—on-ly look and re-ceive.
deem-er, was slain, That they thro' His death might sal-va-tion ob-tain.
off in-to shame, O tell them there's par-don and peace in His name.
wide-ly un-furl'd, An-nounc-ing His king-dom, the theme of the world.

Chorus.

Send out the glad ti-dings, e-ter-ni-ty's near, Sound the call of re-demp-tion, so sweet and so clear; Not for one, but for all, Je - sus

came to a - tone, And we thro' His mer - cy draw nigh to His throne.

61   I am Coming to the Cross.

Rev. W. McDonald.   W. G. Fischer.

1. I am com-ing to the cross; I am poor, and weak, and blind;
2. Long my heart has sigh'd for Thee; Long has e - vil dwelt with - in;
3. Here I give my all to Thee,—Friends, and time, and earth-ly store;

Ref.—*I am trust-ing, Lord, in Thee, Blest Lamb of Cal-va-ry;*

D. C. for Ref.

I am count-ing all but dross; I shall full sal - va - tion find.
Je - sus sweet - ly speaks to me, I will cleanse you from all sin.
Soul and bod - y Thine to be— Wholly Thine for ev - er more.
Hum-bly at Thy cross I bow; Save me, Je - sus, save me now.

63

62 Thy Life was Given for Me.

FRANCES R. HAVERGAL, by per.   IRA D. SANKEY.

1. Thy life was given for me! Thy pre-cious blood, was shed That
2. Long years were spent for me In wear - i - ness and woe, That
3. Thy Fa-ther's home of light, Thy rain - bow - cir - cled throne, Were
4. Oh, let my life be given, My years for Thee be spent; World-

I might ran-somed be, And quickened from the dead. Thy
thro' e - ter - ni - ty Thy glo - ry I might know. Long
left for earth - ly night, For wand'rings sad and lone. Yea,
fet - ters all be riven, And joy with suf-f'ring blent: To

life was giv'n for me (for me): What have I giv'n for Thee (for Thee)?
years were spent for me (for me): Have I spent one for Thee (for Thee)?
all was left for me (for me): Have I left aught for Thee (for Thee)?
Thee my all I bring (I bring): My Sav-iour and my King (my King)!

Thy life, was giv'n for me (for me): What have I giv'n for Thee?
Long years, were spent for me (for me): Have I spent one for Thee?
Yea all, was left for me (for me): Have I left aught for Thee?
To Thee my all I bring (I bring): My Sav-iour and my King!

6-1

63   In Pastures Green.

GRACE J. FRANCES.   HUBERT P. MAIN.

1. In pas-tures green He lead-eth me, My falt-'ring steps He guides;
2. In pas-tures green He lead-eth me, Where healthful wa-ters flow;
3. In pas-tures green He lead-eth me, To Him my voice I'll raise,
4. In pas-tures green He lead-eth me, No ill my soul shall fear;

And for my need how gra-cious-ly My Shepherd still pro-vides.
He spreads His ban-ner o-ver me, My shield from ev-ery foe.
Whose lov-ing kindness ten-der-ly Has fol-lowed all my days.
His rod and staff shall com-fort me, For He is ev-er near.

Refrain.

He lead-eth me, He lead-eth me, My soul with gladness sings;

While safe I rest, se-cure and blest, Be-neath His might-y wings.

64   Our Pledge.

GRACE J. FRANCES.   HUBERT P. MAIN.

1. Our will - ing serv - ice, Lord, to Thee, We pledge ourselves to give,
2. We pledge ourselves with fil - ial love To fol - low Thy com-mands,
3. And so we pledge ourselves to walk, That those a-round may see,

For Thou hast bought us with Thy blood, And died that we might live;
To aid the Church by word and deed, And stay our pas-tor's hands;
The calm re - flec - tion of a light That on - ly shines from Thee;

We pledge ourselves by grace to yield O - be - dience to Thy laws,
Be this our one su - preme de - sire, Our pur-pose, thought and aim,
O help us, Lord, our pledge to keep; We need Thy con-stant care,

De - vo - tion to Thy sa - cred truth, Thy kingdom and Thy cause.
In what - so - ev - er we shall do, To glo - ri - fy Thy name.
To guard our hearts from ev - ery sin, Our feet from ev - ery snare.

65   What will You do with Jesus?

JULIA STERLING.

IRA D. SANKEY.

1. What will you do with Je - sus? Think well ere you de - cide;
2. What will you do with Je - sus? He's knocking at your heart;
3. What will you do with Je - sus, Your on - ly hope of heav'n,

Once came the fa - tal an - swer:—Let Him be cru - ci - fied.
Will you ad - mit the Sav - iour, Or shall He now de - part?
If you should die with - out Him, Unblessed and un - for - giv'n?

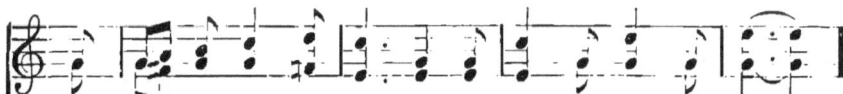

And will you slight His mer - cy, And cru - ci - fy a - gain,
What will you say to Je - sus? Will you re - ject His love?
O, nev - er could you en - ter The pearl - y gate so fair,

The Lord of life and glo - ry, For your re - demp-tion slain?
Can this vain world, so transient, Give joy like that a - bove?
That o - pens to the king-dom, Where ma-ny man-sions are.

66 Christ and the Church.

J. R. CLEMENTS. [FIRST TUNE.] GEO. C. STEBBINS

1. " For Christ and the Church " we stand (we stand), U - nit - ed heart and hand;
2. " For Christ and the Church " we pray (we pray), And la - bor day by day,
3. " For Christ and the Church " we sing (we sing), And glad ho - san - nas bring;

Our lips His praise to speak, Our hands to help the weak;..
With zeal and cour - age new We'll strive some work to do,.....
Since He hath made us free, And prom-ised vic - to - ry,.....

Our feet the lost to seek,... " For Christ (for Christ), and the Church."
And keep our covenant true,... " For Christ (for Christ), and the Church."
Our mot - to still shall be,..... " For Christ (for Christ), and the Church."

Chorus.

" For Christ.... and the Church " we stand, U - nit - ed heart and hand;
for Christ U - nit - ed heart and

Christic and the Church.—Concluded.

Our lives we give, hence-forth to live "For Christ (for Christ), and the Church."

67   Still, still with Thee.

HARRIET B. STOWE.   IRA D. SANKEY.

1. Still, still with Thee, when pur-ple morn-ing break-eth, When the bird
2. A-lone with Thee, a-mid the mys-tic shad-ows, The sol-emn
3. As in the dawn-ing, o'er the wave-less o-cean, The im-age
4. Still, still to Thee! as to each new-born morn-ing A fresh and

wak-eth, and the shad-ows flee;   Fair-er than morn-ing,
hush of na-ture new-ly-born;   A-lone with Thee in
of the morn-ing-star doth rest;   So in this still-ness,
sol-emn splen-dor still is given,   So does this bless-ed

lov-li-er than day-light, Dawns the sweet consciousness, I am with Thee.
breathless ad-o-ra-tion, In the calm dew and freshness of the morn.
Thou be-hold-est on-ly Thine im-age in the wa-ters of my breast.
consciousness a-wak-ing, Breathe each day nearness unto Thee and heaven.

Copyright, 1894, by The Biglow & Main Co.   69

68 The Anchored Soul.

Rev. W. O. Cushing.

Rev. Robert Lowry.

1. I'm rest-ing se-cure-ly in Je - sus now! I sail the wide
2. O long on the o - cean my bark was toss'd, Where tempests and
3. How sweet in the ha - ven of rest to a - bide! Se - cure from all

seas no more; The tempests may sweep o'er the wild stormy deep—I am
storms ne'er cease; My heart was in fear, and no ref - uge was near, Till in
doubt and fear,—The billows may roll, but there's rest for the soul When the

Chorus.

safe where the storms come no more. ⎫
Je - sus my soul found its peace. ⎬ I've an-chored my soul in the
voice of my Sav - iour I hear. ⎭

ha - ven of rest, I sail the wild seas no more, no more; The

The Anchored Soul.—Concluded.

tempests may sweep o'er the wild, storm-y deep, But in Je - sus I'm

safe ev - er-more, ev-er-more, But in Je - sus I'm safe ev - er - more.

69   Resurrection Morn.

S. BARING-GOULD, by per.   IRA D. SANKEY.

1. On   the Res - ur - rec - tion morning, Soul and bod - y meet a - gain,
2. Here a-while they must be part - ed, And the flesh its Sab - bath keep,
3. For   a space the tir - ed bod - y Waits in peace the morning's dawn,
4. On that hap - py East - er morn-ing All the graves their dead re-store,
5. Soul and bod - y, re - u - nit - ed, Henceforth nothing shall di - vide,

No more sor - row, no more weep - ing. No.... more pain.
Wait - ing in a ho - ly still - ness, Wrapped in sleep.
When there breaks the last and bright- est East - er morn.
Fa - ther, moth - er, sis - ter, broth - er, Meet once more.
Wak - ing up in Christ's own like-ness, Sat - - is - fied.

70   My One Endeavor.

JULIA STERLING.

IRA D. SANKEY.

1. O help me, dear Lord, Thy love to praise, From death to life it brought
2. O help me to make of all I have, A will-ing con-se-cra-
3. O help me to trust, and watch, and pray, Thy pre-cious word be-liev-
4. O help me to do what-e'er Thou wilt, To go where Thou wouldst send

me; And now I sing the glad new song, Thy grace di-vine has taught me.
tion, To spread abroad the joy-ful news Of free and full sal-va-tion.
ing; To walk by faith from day to day, No more Thy Spir-it griev-ing.
me; As-sured of this, my Saviour's hand Will guide and still de-fend me.

Chorus.

Help me to live, O Lord, for Thee, Be this my one en-deav-or,

To glo-ri-fy Thy name on earth, And reign with Thee for-ev-er.

71   Weeping Hours will Soon be Over.

BERTHA MASON.   W. H. DOANE.

1. Weeping hours will soon be o - ver, And a joy will come to the
2. Weeping hours will soon be o - ver, There's a home a - bove ev - er
3. Weeping hours will soon be o - ver, Ev - ery tear be wiped from our
4. Weeping hours will soon be o - ver, All the toils and cares of the

soul at last; Kin-dred ties that here are broken, We shall find when the
bright and fair; We shall all for - get our sor-row In the bliss that a-
eyes a - way; When we know and greet each oth-er In the light of e
world shall cease; Weary days and nights of watching, Will be lost in the

Refrain.

night is o'er.
waits us there.
ter - nal day.
home of peace.

Weeping hours will soon be o - ver, Soon in bonds of

union sweet, With the dear ones gone before us, We shall rest at Jesus feet.

72 With Jesus Everywhere.

Frank W. Hutt.

Chas. H. Gabriel.

1. Lord, I am not my own, but Thine, I would Thine arm - or bear;
2. 'Tis strong for bat - tle I must be, And for my foes pre-pare;
3. If Thou should'st summon me to go, Thy gos - pel to de - clare

And where Thou lead - est I would go, And all Thy triumphs share,
Lord, Thou my great Com-mand-er art, On Thee I'll cast my care,
In hea - then lands, dear Lord, I know Thy grace will guide me there:

For lo! there's vic - to - ry and peace With Je - sus ev - ery-where.
For more than conqu'ror I shall be, With Je - sus ev - ery-where.
And I shall find en - dur - ing love With Je - sus ev - ery-where.

Refrain.

With Je - sus ev - ery-where, With Je - sus ev - ery-where,
With Je - sus   With Je - sus

With Jesus Everywhere.—Concluded.

For lo! there's vic-to-ry and peace, With Je-sus ev-ery-where.
For more than conqu'ror I shall be, With Je-sus ev-ery-where.
And I shall find en-dur-ing love, With Je-sus ev-ery-where.

73   Go Tell it to Jesus.

M. A. BACHELOR, alt.   HARRY S. LOWER.

1. Go bur-y thy sor-row, The world has its share: Go bur-y it
2. Go tell it to Je-sus, He know-eth thy grief; Go tell it to
3. Hearts growing a-wea-ry With heav-i-er woe Now droop 'mid the

deep-ly, Go hide it with care; Go think of it calm-ly, When
Je-sus,—He'll send thee re-lief, Go gath-er the sun-shine He
dark-ness—Go com-fort them, go; Go bur-y thy sor-row, Let

cur-tain'd by night, Go tell it to Je-sus, And all will be right.
sheds on the way; He'll lighten thy bur-den, Go, wea-ry one, pray.
oth-ers be blest; Go give them the sunshine—Tell Je-sus the rest.

74   Keep Step with the Master.

IDA S. TAYLOR.   W. A. OGDEN.

1. Keep step with the Mas-ter, what-ev-er be-tide; Tho dark be the
2. Keep step with the Mas-ter, wher-ev-er you go; Thro' dark-ness, and
3. Keep step with the Mas-ter, nor halt by the way; What-e'er He com-

path-way, keep close to your Guide, While foes are al-lur-ing, and
shad-ow, the way He will show, The light of His pres-ence your
mands you, oh, haste to o-bey! A-rise at His bid-ding, press

dan-ger is near, When walk-ing with Je-sus, you've noth-ing to fear.
path will il-lume, And make all the des-ert a gar-den of bloom.
on in His might; While walk-ing with Je-sus, you're sure to be right.

Chorus.

Keep-ing step (keep-ing step), go brave-ly for-ward, And thy

Keep Step.—Concluded.

cour - - - age still re - new,............ Dai - ly
And thy cour - age still re - new, still re - new,

walk.... with Christ your Saviour, He will lead you all the journey through.
dai - ly walk

75   I Love Thy Kingdom, Lord.

TIMOTHY DWIGHT.   (LABAN. S. M.)   LOWELL MASON.

1. I   love Thy king-dom, Lord, The house of Thine a - bode,
2. I   love Thy Church, O God! Her walls be - fore Thee stand,
3. Be - yond my high - est joy   I   prize her heavenly ways,
4. Sure as   Thy truth shall last, To Zi - on shall be giv'n

The Church our blest Re-deem-er saved With His own pre - cious blood.
Dear as   the ap - ple of Thine eye, And grav - en   on   Thy hand.
Her sweet commun-ion sol - emn vows, Her hymns of love and praise.
The bright-est glo - ries earth can yield, And bright- er bliss of heav'n.

My Hiding Place.

T. RAFFLES.   (QUARTET.)   S. THALBERG, arr.

1. Thou art my hid-ing place, O Lord! In Thee I put my trust;
2. When storms of fierce temp-ta-ion beat, And fu-rious foes as-sail,
3. And when Thine aw-ful voice commands This bod-y to de-cay,

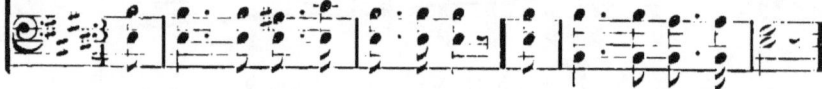

En-cour-aged by Thy ho-ly word, A fee-ble child of dust:
My ref-uge is the mer-cy-seat, My hope, with-in the vail:
And life in its last ling'ring sands, Is ebb-ing fast a-way;—

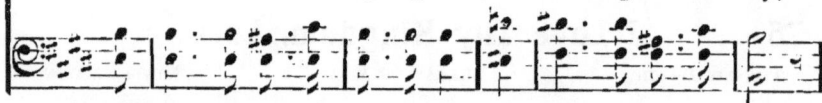

I have no ar-gu-ment be-side, I urge no oth-er plea;
From strife of tongues, and bit-ter words, My spir-it flies to Thee;
Then, tho' it be in ac-cents weak, My voice shall call on Thee,

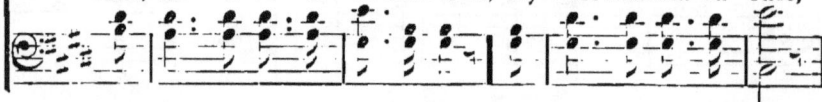

And 'tis enough my Sav-iour died, My Sav-iour died for me!
Joy to my heart the tho't af-fords, My Sav-iour died for me!
And ask for strength in death to speak, "My Sav-iour died for me."

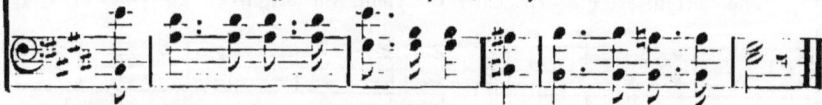

The Bright Forevermore.

F. J. C.

W. A. OGDEN.

1. There is a land, a sun-ny land, Whose skies are ev-er bright;
2. There is a clime, a peace-ful clime, Be-yond life's nar-row sea;
3. There is a home, a glo-rious home, A heav'n-ly man-sion fair;
4. We soon shall leave these fad-ing scenes, That glide so quick-ly by;

Where evening shad-ows nev-er fade, The Sav-iour is its light.
Where ev-ery storm is hush'd to rest, There let our treas-ure be.
And those who lov'd so fond-ly here, Will bid us wel-come there.
And join the shin-ing hosts a-bove, Where joy can nev-er die.

Chorus.

If the cross... we meekly bear,... Then a crown we shall wear,...
If the cross we meek-ly bear, We a gold-en crown shall wear,

When we dwell... a-mong the fair,.... In the bright, for-ev-er-more.
When we dwell a-mong the fair,

79

78 It is Good to be Here.

F. J. CROSBY.   WM. B. BRADBURY, arr.

1. We come once a - gain our Re - deem-er to meet, We turn from the
2. We come where so oft we have gathered be - fore, His bless - ed com-
3. We come in His name, as He taught us to come, Who knows ev - ery

world and its care; To wor-ship the King as we bow at His feet,
mun - ion to share; Our souls to re - fresh at the fountain of grace,
bur - den we bear; Still rest-ing our hope on the strength of His word,

Chorus.

And seek for His bless-ing in prayer.
And seek His di - rect - ion in prayer. } And now may His promise to
We know He will an-swer our prayer.

us be fulfilled, That He in our midst will ap - pear; And then we shall

80

It is Good to be Here.—Concluded.

sing in the full-ness of joy, Praise the Lord, it is good to be here.

79 Help Us to Labor On.

F. J. Crosby.

W. H. Doane.

1. Help us to la-bor on, Sav-iour, for Thee; Faith-ful in
2. Help us to la-bor on, Cheer'd from a-bove; Sow-ing the
3. Help us to la-bor on, Lord, not in vain; O may we

Refrain.

word and deed, O may we be.
word of life, Tell-ing Thy love. } Till all our work is done,
gath-er in, Bright, gold-en grain. }

Our crown of glo-ry won, Help us, Lord, to la-bor on, Trusting in Thee.

81

80   A Stranger at the Door.

JOSEPH GRIGG.

IRA D. SANKEY.

1. Be-hold a Stran-ger at the door! He gen-tly knocks, has knock'd before,
2. O! love-ly at - ti-tude! He stands With melting heart and lad-en hands;
3. But will He prove a friend in-deed? He will, the ver-y friend you need—
4. Rise, touched with grat-i-tude divine, Turn out His en - e - my and thine,

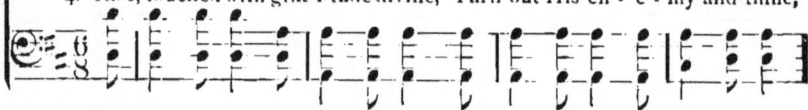

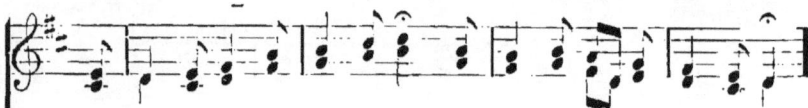

Has wait-ed long, is wait-ing still; You treat no oth-er friend so ill.
Oh! matchless kindness! and He shows This matchless kindness to His foes.
The Friend of sin-ners; yes, 'tis He, With garments dyed on Cal - va - ry.
That soul-de-stroy-ing mon-ster sin, And let the heavenly Stranger in.

Chorus.

Oh, let the dear Saviour come in (come in), He'll cleanse thy heart from sin;

Oh, keep Him no more out-side the door, But let the dear Saviour come in.

81 I Heard the Voice.

HORATIUS BONAR, D.D.   Arr. from L. SPOHR.

1. I heard the voice of Je-sus say, "Come un-to me and rest;
2. I heard the voice of Je-sus say, "Be-hold, I free-ly give
3. I heard the voice of Je-sus say, "I am this dark world's light:

Lay down, thou wea-ry one, lay down Thy head up-on my breast."
The liv-ing wa-ter; thirst-y one, Stoop down, and drink, and live."
Look un-to me; thy morn shall rise, And all thy day be bright."

I came to Je-sus as I was, Wea-ry and worn and sad;
I came to Je-sus, and I drank Of that life-giv-ing stream;
I looked to Je-sus and I found In Him my Star, my Sun;

I found in Him a rest-ing-place, And He has made me glad.
My thirst was quench'd, my soul re-vived, And now I live in Him.
And in that light of life I'll walk Till all my jour-ney's done.

83

82 Send The Light.

C. H. G.

CHAS. H GABRIEL.

1. There's a call comes ring-ing o'er the rest-less wave, "Send the light!...."
2. We have heard the Ma - ce - do - nian call to - day, "Send the light,...."
3. Let us pray that grace may ev - ery-where a-bound, Send the light,....
4. Let us not grow wea - ry in the work of love, Send the light,....

Send the light!

send the light!" There are souls to res-cue, there are souls to save,
send the light!" And a gold en off'ring at the cross we lay,
send the light! And a Christ-like spir - it in our lives be found,
send the light! While we gath er jew-els for a crown a-bove,

send the light!

Chorus.

Send the light!.... send the light!.... Send the light,.... the

Send the light! send the light! Send the light,

bless-ed gos - pel light, Let it shine...... from shore to

the bless - ed gos - pel light, Let it shine

Copyright, 1894, by Geo. F. Rosche. Used by per.

N4

Send The Light.—Concluded.

shore!.......... shine...... for - ev - er - more..........

from shore to shore! Let it shine for - ev - er - more.

83   Like a River Glorious.

F. R. HAVERGAL, by per.   IRA D. SANKEY.

1. Like a riv - er, glo - rious Is God's per - fect peace, O - ver all vic -
2. Hid-den in the hol - low Of His bless - ed hand, Nev - er foe can
3. Ev - ery joy or tri - al Fall-eth from a - bove, Trac'd upon our

to - rious In its bright in - crease. Per - fect—yet it flow - eth
fol - low, Nev-er trai - tor stand. Not a surge of wor - ry,
di - al By the Sun of Love. We may trust Him sole - ly

Full - er ev - ery day; Per - fect—yet it grow - eth Deep - er all the way.
Not a shade of care, Not a blast of hur - ry Touch the spir - it there.
All for us to do; They who trust Him wholly, Find Him whol - ly true.

Copyright, 1894, by The Biglow & Main Co.

85

Onward, Christian Soldiers.

S. Baring-Gould, by per.

A. S. Sullivan.

Presto.

1. On - ward, Chris-tian sol - diers! Marching as to war, Look - ing
2. Like a might - y ar - my Moves the church of God; Broth - ers,
3. Crowns and thrones may per - ish, Kingdoms rise and wane; But the

un - to Je - sus, Who is gone be - fore; Christ, the Roy - al
we are tread - ing Where the saints have trod; We are not di -
church of Je - sus Con - stant will re - main; Gates of hell can

Mas - ter, Leads a - gainst the foe; For-ward in - to bat - tle,
vid - ed, All one bod - y we— One in hope and doc - trine,
nev - er 'Gainst that church prevail; We have Christ's own prom-ise—

Chorus.

See His ban - ners go!
One in char - i - ty. } On-ward, Chris-tian sol - diers! March-ing
And that can - not fail.

Onward, Christian Soldiers.—Concluded.

as to war, Look-ing un-to Je-sus, Who is gone be-fore.

4 Onward then, ye people!
  Join our happy throng;
  Blend with ours your voices
  In the triumph-song;

"Glory, praise, and honor,
  Unto Christ the King,"
This through countless ages
Men and angels sing.

85   As Pants the Hart.

NAHUM TATE.   HUBERT P. MAIN.

1. As pants the hart for cool-ing streams, When heat-ed in the chase,
2. For Thee, my God—the liv-ing God, My thirst-y soul doth pine;
3. I sigh to think of hap-pier days, When Thou, O Lord! wast nigh;
4. Why rest-less, why cast down, my soul? Hope still; and thou shalt sing

So longs my soul, O God, for Thee, And Thy re-fresh-ing grace.
Oh, when shall I be-hold Thy face, Thou Maj-es-ty di-vine!
When ev-ery heart was tuned to praise, And none more blest than I.
The praise of Him who is thy God, Thy health's e-ter-nal spring.

86 Moment by Moment.

D. W. WHITTLE.

MARY WHITTLE.

1. Dy - ing with Je - sus, by death reck-oned mine; Liv - ing with
2. Nev - er a tri - al that He is not there, Nev - er a
3. Nev - er a heart-ache, and nev - er a groan, Nev - er a
4. Nev - er a weakness that He doth not feel, Nev - er a

Je - sus, a new life di - vine; Look - ing to Je - sus 'till
bur - den that He doth not bear, Nev - er a sor - row that
tear-drop and nev - er a moan; Nev - er a dan - ger but
sick-ness that He can - not heal; Mo - ment by mo - ment, in

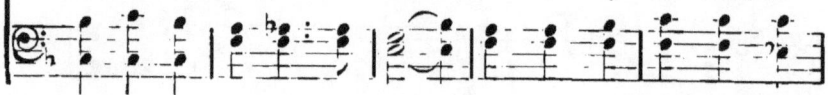

glo - ry doth shine, Mo-ment by mo - ment, O Lord, I am Thine.
He doth not share, Mo-ment by mo - ment I'm un - der His care.
there on the throne, Mo-ment by mo - ment He thinks of His own.
woe or in weal, Je - sus, my Sav - iour, a - bides with me still.

Chorus.

Mo - ment by mo - ment I'm kept in His love; Mo - ment by

Moment by Moment.—Concluded.

mo-ment I've life from a - bove; Look-ing to Je - sus till

glo - ry doth shine; Mo-ment by mo - ment, Oh, Lord, I am Thine.

87   If, On a Quiet Sea.

A. M. TOPLADY.   (TENDERNESS. S. M.)   E. HAMILTON.

Moderato.

1. If,   on a   qui - et   sea,   Tow'rd heav'n we calm-ly   sail,
2. But should the   sur - ges   rise,   And   rest de - lay to   come,
3. Soon shall our   doubts and fears   All   yield to Thy con - trol:

With grate-ful hearts, O God, to Thee, We'll own the fav - 'ring gale.
Blest be   the sor - row, kind the storm, Which drives us near-er   home.
Thy ten - der mer - cies shall il - lume The mid-night of the   soul.

88   Drifting Away.

F. J. CROSBY.

IRA D. SANKEY.

ad libitum.

1. Out on the bil-low, lur'd by the temp-ter, Griev-ing the lov'd ones by
2. Out on the bil-low, still thou art drift-ing, Far-ther and far-ther a-
3. Out on the bil-low, lone-ly and wea-ry, Conscious of dan-ger, O
4. Fly then to Je-sus, trust in His mer-cy, Hear the glad message, O

night and by day; Turn thee, O lost one, dream-ing of pleas-ure,
way on the tide; Clouds in the dis-tance, dark-ness a-round thee,
why wilt thou roam? Lov'd ones are watch-ing, ear-nest-ly long-ing,
hear and o-bey—"I am thy Ref-uge, Rock, and Sal-va-tion,

Why art thou drift-ing, still drift-ing a-way?
No one to help thee, and no one to guide.
Ea-ger-ly wait-ing to wel-come thee home.
I will re-ceive thee; why lon-ger de-lay?"

Refrain.

Drift-ing a-way,

drift-ing a-way, Far-ther from hope and farther a-stray; Out of the light,

Drifting Away.—Concluded.

in - to the night, Why art thou drift-ing, still drift-ing a-way?

89   I Know Not What to Ask.

F. J. CROSBY.   H. P. DANKS.

1. I know not what to   ask,   O Sav - iour mine; Be this my ear - nest
2. I know not what is   best,   But Thou can'st see; Then let me leave it
3. I know not where the path That I should tread, Un-less Thy gracious

pray'r, O keep me Thine; Hold Thou my trembling hand, That I may
all,   My Lord, to Thee; Whate'er Thy mer-cy grants, Or love de -
light   Is o'er me shed; I   know not if this hour My last may

know Thou art be-side me still, Where'er I go (Where'er I go).
nies, My faith shall turn to Thee Her grate-ful eyes (Her grate-ful eyes).
be,   But this, O Lord, I know, 'Tis well with me ('Tis well with me).

91

90 Young Men, Arise.

Rev. J. H. Edwards.   Rev. Robert Lowry.

1. "A - rise, young men, a - rise!" Thy Sav - iour's lov - ing voice
2. A - rise! for death is nigh, Life's day is all too brief;
3. A - rise from dreams of fame, From sen - sual slum - ber rise;

Now bids thee lift thine eyes, And in His life re - joice;
Like light its mo-ments fly, Its glad - ness and its grief;
Keep spot-less Christ's dear name, Thy wealth seek in the skies;

He raised the sleep - ing dead, And made it grand to live;
A - rise, and take thy part, In God's tre - mend - ous fight;
The no - blest works a wait Thine aid with high re - ward,

For thee His blood was shed, All help His arm will give.
To arms! stir up thy heart, Go forth in heaven's great might.
And, crowned at glo - ry's gate, Thou'lt meet thy ris - en Lord.

92

91 How Sweet the Hour.

F. J. CROSBY.

Scotch Air.

Moderato.

1. How sweet the hour of praise and pray'r, When our de - vo - tions blend,
2. How sweet the tie of hal - lowed love That binds our hearts in one;
3. Yes, soon our worn, and wea - ry feet Will reach the gold - en strand,

And on the wings of faith di - vine, Our songs of joy as - cend;
When gath - ered in the bless - ed name Of Christ, the Fa - ther's Son.
Where those we love, our com - ing wait, In yon - der sum - mer land;

'Tis then we hear in tones more clear The gra - cious prom - ise given,
And though the part - ing soon may come, Yet in His Word is given,
A few more days, a few more years, By storm and temp - est driven,
CHO.—*We all shall meet in heav'n at last, We all shall meet in heaven;*

D. S. for CHO.

That though we part from friends on earth, We all shall meet in heaven.
The bless - ed hope that by and by, We all shall meet in heaven.
With songs, and ev - er - last - ing joy, We all shall meet in heaven.
Thro' faith in Je - sus' pre - cious blood, We all shall meet in heaven.

92 Endeavorer's Marching Song.

F. J. CROSBY.
IRA D. SANKEY.

1. Christ-ian sol-diers all, hear our Leader's call, Who will ral-ly at the
2. Hear the trump of war, sound-ing near and far, Haste to con-quer in Je-
3. On, our foes to brave; on, the world to save; Arm'd with courage, as the
4. When our la-bor done, and the vic-t'ry won, Then with Je-sus we shall

King's com-mand? Firm-ly, stead-i-ly, on to vic-to-ry,
ho - vah's name; To the prom-ised land, with His might-y hand,
mo - ments fly; Shouts of tri-umph rise, rank to rank re-plies,
meet a - bove; O how sweet 'twill be, there His face to see,

Chorus.

See, ad - vanc-ing, "Our En-deav - or Band."
He will lead us with a loud ac-claim.
As with joy we wave our ban-ners high.
In the man-sions of e - ter - nal love.
} Forward! soldiers, all,

hear our Leader's call, Onward! onward with the Sword and Shield; Sig-nals

Endeavorer's Marching Song.—Concluded.

flash ing bright, in the shin-ing light, Cheer us on-ward to the bat-tle field.

93 Hear Me, Blessed Jesus.

Words arr.   J. H. BURKE.

1. Hear me, bless-ed Je - sus, Bid all fear de - part; Let Thy Spir-it
2. Let me ful - ly trust Thee, Rest-ing on Thy Word; Let me still with
3. Hid-ing in the shad-ow Of Thy shelt'ring wings, I shall rest con-

Chorus.

whis - per Peace with-in my heart.
pa - tience Wait on Thee, O Lord.   } Then, what-e'er Thou send - est,
fid - ing In the King of kings.

Hap-py shall I be, Je-sus, my Re-deem-er, Look-ing un - to Thee.

Copyright, 1891, by The Biglow & Main Co.

95

Send the Tidings.

F. J Crosby.   W. A. Ogden.

1. Send the ti - dings of sal - va - tion, Far and wide to ev - ery clime;
2. While the lines to us have fall - en In a good - ly pleas-ant land,
3. While with cheerful hearts we gath - er In the homes to us so dear,

Let the morn-ing rise in splen-dor, Prom-ised long in old - en time.
May we bring our gifts be - fore Thee, Lay them down with will-ing hand;
Ma - ny bow them-selves to i - dols That can nei - ther see nor hear;

Love - ly morn of Zi - on's glo - ry, When her chil-dren now oppress'd,
Send the glo-rious news of par - don, In - to realms of deep - est night;
Speed, O speed the bless - ed mes-sage, Sound a - broad the Sav-iour's fame,

Shall be gath-er'd, out of bondage From the East and from the West.
Tell the souls that sit in dark-ness Je - sus came to bring them light.
Go ye forth and preach the gos - pel Go ye forth in Je - sus name.

95   Never say Good-Bye.

F. J. CROSBY.   IRA D. SANKEY.

1. O   blessed home where those who meet Shall nev-er   say good-bye;
2. Be - yond this vale of toil and care, We'll nev-er say good-bye;
3. When safe a-mong the ransomed throng, We'll nev-er say good-bye;
4. On yon - der fair and peace-ful shore—We'll nev-er say good-bye;

Where kindred souls each oth - er greet, And nev - er say good - bye.
We   part   in tears on earth, but there—We'll nev - er say good - bye.
Where life is one e - ter - nal song, We'll nev - er say good - bye.
But dwell with Christ for-ev - er - more, And nev - er say good - bye.

Chorus.

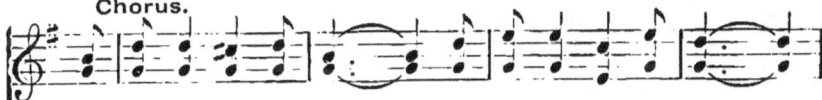

We'll nev - er say good - bye,.... We'll nev - er say good - bye;....
            good-bye,   good-bye;

In that fair land be - yond the sky, We'll nev - er say good - bye.

Blessed Redeemer.

JULIA STERLING.

GEO. C. STEBBINS.

1. Bless-ed Re-deem-er, thro' faith in Thy name, This our en-deav or the
2. Help us to teach them the truths we have heard, Help us to point them to
3. Quick-ly the mo-ments are pass-ing a - way, Let us be ear - nest and

lost to re - claim, Souls for Thy kingdom of glo - ry to win. Out of the
Thee thro' Thy word; Help us to show them that Thou art the Way, Grant us this
work while we may; Work till the summer and harvest are o'er, Then with the

Chorus.

high-ways and hedg-es of sin. }
pow'r Lord, we ear-nest - ly pray. } Blessed Re-deem - er, thro' faith in Thy
reap - ers re-joice ev - er - more. }

name, This our en-deav-or the lost to re-claim; Lifting their bur-dens of

Blessed Redeemer.—Concluded.

sor-row and woe, Cheer-ing the lone - ly wher-ev - er we go.

97   Keep Thou My Way.

F. J. CROSBY.   THEO. E. PERKINS.

1. Keep Thou my way, O Lord, Be Thou ev - er nigh; Strong is Thy
2. Keep Thou my heart, O Lord, Ev - er close to Thee; Safe in Thine
3. Keep Thou my all, O Lord, Hide my life in Thine; O let Thy

might-y arm, Weak and frail am I; Thou my unchanging Friend,
arms of love, Shall my ref - uge be; Then o'er a tran-quil tide,
sa - cred light, O'er my path-way shine; Kept by Thy ten - der care,

On Thee my hopes depend, Till life's brief day shall end, Be Thou ev-er nigh.
My bark shall safe-ly glide, I shall be sat - is - fied, Ev-er close to Thee.
Gladly the cross I'll bear, Hear Thou and grant my pray'r, Hide my life in Thine.

98 Believe and Obey.

JULIA STERLING.   IRA D. SANKEY.

1. Press on-ward, press on-ward, and trust-ing the Lord Re-mem-ber the
2. Press on-ward, press on-ward, if you would se-cure The rest of the
3. Press on-ward, press on-ward, your cour-age re-new; The prize is be-

prom-ise pro-claim'd in His word; He guid-eth the foot-steps, di-
faith-ful, a-bid-ing and sure; The gift of sal-va-tion is
fore you, the crown is in view, His love is so bound-less, He'll

rect-eth the way Of all who con-fess Him, be-lieve, and o-bey.
of-fer'd to-day To all who con-fess Him, be-lieve, and o-bey.
nev-er say nay To those who con-fess Him, be-lieve, and o-bey.

Chorus.

Be-lieve and o-bey, be-lieve and o-bey; The Mas-ter is

Believe and Obey.—Concluded.

call - ing, no lon - ger de - lay: The light of His mer - cy shines

bright on the way Of all who con - fess Him, be - lieve, and o - bey.

99   Blessed Day.

F. J. CROSBY.   (A SABBATH HYMN.)   D. E. JONES.

1. Bless-ed day, when pure de - vo - tions Rise to God on wings of love;
2. Bless-ed day, when bells are call - ing Wea - ry souls from earth-ly care;
3. Bless-ed day, so calm and rest-ful, Bringing joy and peace to all;
4. Bless-ed day, thy light is fad - ing, One by one its beams de - part;

When we catch the dis-tant mu - sic Of the an - gel choirs a - bove.
And we come with hearts up - lift - ed, To the ho - ly place of pray'r.
Lin - ger yet in tran-quil beau - ty, Ere the shades of ev - 'ning fall.
May their calm and sweet re - flec - tion Still a - bide in ev - ery heart.

O Golden Day.

Rev. C. A. Dickenson.   Hubert P. Main.

* 1. O gold - en day so long desired, Born of a darksome night,
2. The nois - es of the night shall cease, The storms no lon - ger roar;
3. Sing on, ye cho - rus of the morn, Your grand En-deav-or strain,

The swinging globe at last is fired By thy re-splendent light.
The fac - tious foes of God's own peace Shall vex His church no more.
Till Christian hearts, estranged and torn, Blend in the glad re - frain;

And Hark! like Memnon's morning chord, Is heard from sea to sea
A thou-sand, thou-sand voic - es sing In surg - ing har - mo - ny:
And all the church, with all its pow'rs, In lov - ing loy - al - ty

This song: One Mas-ter, Christ, the Lord; And brethren all are we.
This song: One Mas-ter, Sav - iour, King; And brethren all are we.
Shall sing: One Mas-ter, Christ, is ours; And brethren all are we.

* These words may be used to tune on following page.
Copyright, 1893, by The Biglow & Main Co.

101 Our Best and Truest Friend.

F. J. CROSBY. (ELLACOMBE.) German.

1. Once more we lift our wait - ing eyes, O gracious Lord, to Thee,
2. Thro' all the past, Thy gen - tle hand Has led us day by day,
3. We thank Thee, Lord, for ev - ery gift Thy grace di - vine be - stows,

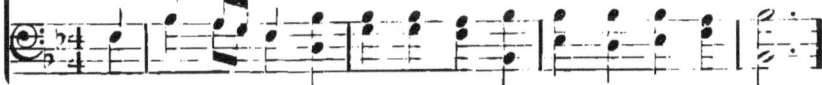

And hum - bly ask that in our midst Thy pres-ence now may be;
Thy pre - cious word with promise sweet, Has cheer'd us on our way;
For peace that calms our troubled souls, And like a riv - er flows;

From earth-ly toil we turn a - side, An - oth - er hour to spend,
We praise Thy name while here a - gain Be - fore Thy throne we bend,
O guard our lives, in - spire our songs, Our on-ward steps de - fend,

In blest com mun-ion at Thy throne, Our best, and tru - est Friend.
To wor - ship Thee with all our hearts, Our best, and tru - est Friend.
Till we shall meet in that bright world, Where praise shall never end.

102 Sweet Peace, the Gift of God's Love.

P. H. ROBLIN.

PETER BILHORN.

1. There comes to my heart one sweet strain (sweet strain), A glad and a
2. Thro' Christ on the cross peace was made (was made), My debt by His
3. When Je - sus as Lord I had crown'd (had crown'd), My heart with this
4. In Je - sus at peace I a - bide (a - bide), And while I keep

joy ous re frain (re - frain), I sing it a - gain and a - gain, Sweet
death was all paid (all paid), No oth - er foun - da - tion is laid For
peace did a-bound (a - bound) In Him a rich bless-ing I found, Sweet
close to His side (His side), There's nothing but peace can be - tide, Sweet

Chorus.

peace, the gift of God's love.
peace, the gift of God's love.
peace, the gift of God's love.
peace, the gift of God's love.

Peace, peace, sweet peace, Wonderful gift from a-

bove   Oh, wonderful, wonderful peace, Sweet peace, the gift of God's love.
a-bove,

Rit.

103 Welcome! Wanderer, Welcome!

Horatius Bonar, D. D.   Ira D. Sankey.

1. In the land of stran-gers, Whither thou art gone, Hear a far voice
2. "From the land of hun-ger, Fainting, famished, lone, Come to love and
3. "Leave the haunts of ri - ot, Wast-ed, woe-be-gone, Sick at heart, and

Chorus.

call-ing, "My son! my son!"
glad-ness, My son! my son!" } "Welcome! wand'rer wel-come! wel-come
wea-ry, My son! my son!"

back to home! Thou hast wandered far a-way: Come home! come home!"

4 "See the door still open!
   Thou art still my own;
   Eyes of love are on thee:
   My son! my son!"

5 "Far off thou hast wandered,
   Wilt thou farther roam?
   Come, and all is pardoned,
   My son! my son!"

6 "See the well-spread table,
   Unforgotten one!
   Here is rest and plenty,
   My son! my son!

7 "Thou art friendless, homeless,
   Hopeless, and undone;
   Mine is love unchanging,
   My son! my son!"

104 There is Never a Day so Dreary.

LILLA M. ALEXANDER.   GEO. C. STEBBINS.

1. There is nev-er a day so drear-y, But God can make it
2. There is nev-er a cross so heav-y, But the nail-scar'd hands are
3. There is nev-er a life so dark-en'd, So hope-less and un-

bright; And un-to the soul that trusts Him, He
there, Out-stretched in ten-der com-pas-sion The
blest, But may be fill'd with the light of God, And

giv-eth songs in the night. There is nev-er a path so
bur-den to help us bear. There is nev-er a heart so
en-ter His prom-ised rest. There is nev-er a sin or

hid-den, But God will lead the way, If we seek for the
bro-ken, But the lov-ing Lord can heal; For the heart that was
sor-row, There is nev-er a care or loss, But that we may

There is Never a Day.—Concluded.

Spir - it's guid-ance, And pa - tient - ly wait and pray, If we
pierc'd on Cal - v'ry, Doth still for His loved ones feel, For the
bring to Je - sus, And leave at the foot of the cross, But

seek for the Spir - it's guid-ance, And pa - tient - ly wait and pray.
heart that was pierc'd on Cal - v'ry, Doth still for His loved ones feel.
that we may bring to Je - sus, And leave at the foot of the cross.

105 Old Hundred. L. M.

Rev. Thomas Ken. (DOXOLOGY.) L. Bourgeois.

Praise God from whom all blessings flow, Praise Him, all creatures here be - low;

Praise Him a - bove, ye heav'n-ly host; Praise Father, Son and Ho - ly Ghost.

106 Thy Word is a Lamp.

GRACE J. FRANCES.   HUBERT P. MAIN.

1. Thy word is a lamp to my feet, O Lord, Thy
2. Thy word is a lamp to my feet, O Lord, And,
3. Thy word is a lamp to my feet, O Lord, And

word is a light to my way; It shines in my soul like a
trust-ing in Thee as my all, What-ev - er of e - vil may
O, when Thy glo - ry I see, For all the rich bless-ings its

star by night, And com - forts and cheers me by day.
cross my path, I nev - er, no, nev - er can fall.
truth has brought, The praise will I give un - to Thee.

Chorus.

O won-der-ful, won-der-ful Word, My treas-ure, my hope, and my stay;

Thy Word is a Lamp.—Concluded.

Each prom-ise recorded brings joy to my soul, And brightens each step of my way.

107 A Missionary Hymn.

F. J Crosby.   Ira D. Sankey.

Moderato.

1. Great Je - ho - vah, might-y Lord, Vast and boundless is Thy word;
2. Jew and Gen - tile, bond and free, All shall yet be one in Thee;
3. From her night shall Chi - na wake, Af - ric's sons their chains shall break;

King of kings, from shore to shore Thou shalt reign for - ev - er - more.
All con - fess Mes - si - ah's name, All His won-drous love pro-claim.
E - gypt, where Thy peo - ple trod, Shall a - dore and praise our God.

4 India's groves of palm so fair,
Shall resound with praise and prayer;
Ceylon's isle with joy shall sing
Glory be to Christ our King.

5 North and South shall own Thy sway,
East and West Thy voice obey,
Crowns and thrones before Thee fall,
King of kings and Lord of all.

Copyright, 1891, by The Biglow & Main Co

108 Speed Away.

F. J. CROSBY.

I. B. WOODBURY, arr.

1. Speed a - way, speed a - way on your mis - sion of light,
2. Speed a - way, speed a - way with the life - giv - ing Word,
3. Speed a - way, speed a - way with the mes - sage of rest,

To the lands that are ly - ing in dark - ness and night; 'Tis the
To the na - tions that know not the voice of the Lord; Take the
To the souls by the tempt-er in bond - age op-press'd; For the

Mas-ter's command; go ye forth in His name, The won - der - ful
wings of the morn-ing and fly o'er the wave, In the strength of your
Sav - iour has purchas'd their ran-som from sin, And the ban - quet is

Gos - pel of Je - sus pro - claim; Take your lives in your hand, to the
Mas - ter the lost ones to save; He is call - ing once more, not a
read - y, O gath - er them in; To the res - cue make haste, there's no

Speed Away.—Concluded.

work while 'tis day, Speed a - way, speed a - way, speed a - way.
mo - ment's de - lay, Speed a - way, speed a - way, speed a - way.
time for de - lay, Speed a - way, speed a - way, speed a - way.

109 In the Cross of Christ.

J. BOWRING. (RATHBUN. 8, 7.) ITHAMAR CONKEY.

1. In the cross of Christ I glo - ry, Tow'ring o'er the
2. When the woes of life o'er-take me, Hopes de - ceive and

wrecks of time; All the light of sa - cred sto - ry,
fears an - noy, Nev - er shall the cross for - sake me;

Gath-ers round its head sub - lime.
Lo! it glows with peace and joy.

3 When the sun of bliss is beaming
  Light and love upon my way,
From the cross the radiance stream-
Adds new lustre to the day. [ing,

4 Bane and blessing, pain and pleas-
  By the cross are sanctified; [ure,
Peace is there, that knows no meas-
Joys that thro' all time abide. [ure,

110   Tell it Out with Loud Hosannas.

F. J. CROSBY.   IRA D. SANKEY.

1. Tell it out with loud ho-san-nas that Je-ho-vah reigns; Tell it
2. Tell it out with hal-le-lu-jahs! like a trum-pet call, Tell it
3. Tell it out up-on the mountains, with tri-umphant voice, Tell it

out (tell it out), Tell it out (tell it out)! He shall free the cap-tive
out (tell it out), Tell it out (tell it out)! That the ban-quet now is
out (tell it out), Tell it out (tell it out)! That the wea-ry, brok-en

na-tions and shall break their chains; Tell it out (tell it out), Tell it out!
read-y, and there's room for all, Tell it out (tell it out), Tell it out!
heart-ed may in Him re-joice; Tell it out (tell it out), Tell it out!

Chorus.

Tell it out a-mong the peo-ple, with a joy-ful sound, 'Till the
Send a-broad the bless-ed ti-dings on the wind's glad wings, That the
Tell it out with joy and glad-ness that the lost may come, To the

Tell it Out with Loud Hosannas.—Concluded.

world shall hear the ech-o to its ut-most bound; Tell it out with ac-cla-
Babe of Bethlehem's manger is the King of kings; Tell it out with ac-cla-
home of ma-ny mansions for there yet is room; Tell it out with ac-cla-

ma-tion that Je-ho-vah reigns, Tell it out (tell it out)! Tell it out!

111   One in Spirit.

GRACE J. FRANCES.   HUBERT P. MAIN.

Andante.

1. Je-sus, Sav-iour, we have prom-ised Thine and on-ly Thine to be;
2. Oh, in-struct us in the wis-dom And the knowledge of Thy ways;
3. May the bless-ed Ho-ly Spir-it From Thy presence now de-scend;

cres.

Guard and keep us firm and stead-fast, One in Spir-it, one in Thee.
Help us fol-low Thy ex-am-ple And be faith-ful all our days.
Fill-ing all our hearts with gladness, While our songs in rapt-ure blend.

112 Wheat and Tares.

W. L., arr.

GEO. C. STEBBINS.

1. Grow - ing to - geth - er, wheat and tares, All clus - ter - ing
2. Grow - ing to - geth - er side by side, And both shall the
3. But O the tares,—for them the word Of a ter - ri - ble

fair and green, Fann'd by the gen - tle sum-mer airs Be -
reap - ers meet— The tares a - loft in their scornful pride, And
doom is cast; "Bind and burn," is the Lord's command, They shall

neath one sky se - rene; O - ver them both the sun - light
bow - ing heads of wheat. Swift and sure o'er the wav - ing
leave the wheat at last; Nev - er a - gain the sum - mer

falls, And o - ver them both the rain, Till the an - gels
plain The sick - le sharp will fly, And the pre - cious
rain, And nev - er the sun - shine sweet, That were lav-ished

Wheat and Tares.—Concluded.

come when the Mas - ter calls To gath - er the gold - en grain.
wheat, the a - bund-ant grain, Be har-vest - ed in the sky.
free - ly, all in vain On the tares a - mong the wheat.

4 Where shall the reapers look for us
When that day of days shall come?
O solemn the thought with grandeur fraught,
Of that wondrous harvest-home!
O Saviour grant when Thine angels come
To reap the fields for Thee,
That we may be found with the golden grain
That garnered in heaven shall be.

113 Ye Christian Heralds! Go.

ANON.　　　(MISSIONARY CHANT. L. M.)　　H. C. ZEUNER.

1. Ye Christian heralds! go, proclaim Sal-va-tion thro' Im-man - uel's name;
2. He'll shield you with a wall of fire, With flaming zeal your breast in - spire,
3. And when our la-bors all are o'er, Then we shall meet to part no more,—

To dis-tant climes the tidings bear, And plant the Rose of Sha-ron there.
Bid raging winds their fu-ry cease, And hush the tempest in - to peace.
With all the ransomed host to fall, And crown our Saviour—Lord of all.

115

114   Saved To-Night.

Rev. E. A. Fridenhagen.   Ira D. Sankey.

1. Down in - to my lone - li - ness, sor - row and night, Il - lu - ming my
2. For years in the dark-ness of sin I have trod, Neg - lect - ing my
3. I'm com - ing in weakness, my Sav - iour, to Thee, From sin and its
4. The mes - sage of par - don at last I have heard, And take Thee as

soul with its ra - di-ance bright; There comes a sweet mes - sage of
Sav - iour, de - spis - ing His blood; A - way from my home, and a -
bond-age I long to be free; Re - ceive me O Mas - ter, Thine
Sav - iour, Re - deem - er and Lord; I'll doubt Thee no lon - ger, but

love and of light, That I may be saved to - night.
way from my God, Yet I may be saved to - night.
own would I be, And I shall be saved to - night.
trust in Thy word, That I may be saved to - night.

Refrain.

That I may be saved to - night, That I may be saved to night;
Yet I may be saved to - night, Yet I may be saved to - night;
And I shall be saved to - night, And I shall be saved to - night;
That I may be saved to - night, That I may be saved to - night;

   116

Saved To-Night.—Concluded.

There comes the sweet word of love and light, That I may be saved to - night.
A - way from my home, my friends, my God, Yet I may be saved to - night.
Re - ceive me O Lord, Thine own to be; And I shall be saved to - night.
I'll doubt Thee no more, but trust Thy word, That I may be saved to - night.

115   Praise Ye the Father.

ANON.

F. F. FLEMMING.

1. Praise ye the Fa - ther, for His lov - ing kind-ness, Ten - der - ly
2. Praise ye the Sav - iour, great is His com - pas - sion, Gra-cious - ly
3. Praise ye the Spir - it, Com fort - er of Is - rael, Sent of the

cares He for His lov - ing chil - dren; Praise Him, ye an - gels,
cares He for His chos - en peo - ple; Young men and maid - ens,
Fa - ther and the Son to bless us; Praise ye the Fa - ther,

praise Him in the heav - ens, Praise ye Je - ho - vah!
ye old men and chil - dren, Praise ye the Sav - iour!
Son, and Ho - ly Spir - it, Praise ye the Tri - une God!

117

116

Who, Who will Go?

Geo. C. Stebbins.

1. Who, who will go to bind the bro-ken heart? Burden'd with grief and
2. Who, who will go to wipe a-way the tear From eyes long used to
3. Who, who will go to seek the lambs a-stray? To lift the fall-en

heav-y in its woe, Long-ing to find in life some bet-ter part,
sor-row's bri-ny flow? To com-fort those who stand beside hope's bier,
where he lies so low, In-to the sun-light of the heav'nly way,

Refrain.

Who, who will go to bind the bro-ken heart? Lord, here am I; send
Who, who will go to wipe a-way the tear? Lord, here am I; send
Who, who will go to seek the lambs a-stray? Lord, here am I; send

me!... send me! To bind the bro-ken heart? To find the
me!... send me! To wipe a-way the tear To stand be
me!... send me! To seek the lambs a-stray? To point the

Copyright, 1894, by The Biglow & Main Co.

118

Who, Who will Go?—Concluded.

Rit.

bet - ter part: Lord, here am I;... send me!... send me!
side hope's bier, Lord, here am I;... send me!... send me!
heav-'nly way,   Lord, here am I;... send me!... send me!

117   All Hail the Power.

Rev. E. PERRONET.   (CORONATION. C. M.)   OLIVER HOLDEN.

1. All hail the pow'r of Je - sus' name! Let an - gels pros-trate fall;
2. Let ev - ery kin-dred, ev - ery tribe, On this ter - res-trial ball,
3. Oh, that with yon - der sa - cred throng We at His feet may fall;

Bring forth the roy - al di - a - dem, And crown Him Lord of all;
To Him all maj - es - ty as - cribe, And crown Him Lord of all;
We'll join the ev - er - last-ing song, And crown Him Lord of all;

Bring forth the roy - al di - a - dem, And crown Him Lord... of all.
To Him all maj - es - ty as - cribe, And crown Him Lord... of all.
We'll join the ev - er - last-ing song, And crown Him Lord... of all.

119

118 Saved by Grace.

F. J. CROSBY.

GEO. C. STEBBINS.

✻ **Duet.**

1. Some day the sil - ver cord will break, And I no more as now shall sing;
2. Some day, when fades the golden sun Beneath the ro - sy-tint - ed west,
3. Some day; till then I ll watch and wait, My lamp all trimm'd and burning bright,
4. Some day my earth - ly house will fall, I can-not tell how soon 'twill be,

But, O, the joy when I shall wake Within the pal-ace of the King!
My blessed Lord shall say, "Well done!" And I shall enter in - to rest.
That when my Saviour opes the gate, My soul to Him may take its flight.
But this I know—My All in All Has now a place in heav'n for me.

Refrain.

rit.

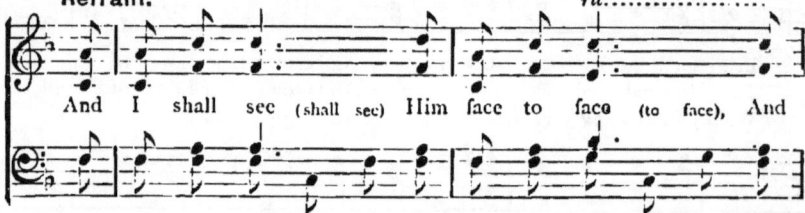

And I shall see (shall see) Him face to face (to face), And

a tempo.

tell the sto - ry—Saved by grace; And I shall see (shall see) Him

✻ If Refrain is sung as Duet, Alto sing first three lines of Tenor an Octave higher.

120

Saved by Grace.—Concluded.

rit .... tempo.

face to face (to face), And tell the sto - ry— Saved by grace.

rit.

---

119   Lord Jesus, Thou dost Keep.

JEAN S. PIGOTT, by per.   (MERIBAH. 8, 6.)   DR. LOWELL MASON.

1. Lord Jesus, Thou dost keep Thy child Thro' sunshine or thro' tempests wild;
2. O glorious Saviour! Thee I praise; To Thee my new glad song I raise,
3. Up - on Thy prom-is-es I stand, Trusting in Thee; Thine own right hand
4. Love per - fect-eth what it be-gins; Thy pow'r doth save me from my sins;

Je - sus, I trust in Thee: Thine is such wondrous pow'r to save,
And tell of what Thou art. Thy grace is boundless in its store;
Doth keep and com - fort me! My soul doth tri-umph in Thy word:
Thy grace up - hold-eth me. This life of trust, how glad, how sweet;

Thine is the might-y love that gave, Its all on Cal - va - ry.
Thy face of love shines ev - er - more, Thou giv-est me Thy heart.
Thine, Thine be all the praise, dear Lord, As Thine the vic - to - ry.
My need, and Thy great ful - ness meet, And I have all in Thee.

120 The Wondrous Cross.

Isaac Watts, arr.

Ira D. Sankey.

1. When I sur-vey.......... the wond-rous cross,..........
2. For-bid it Lord,.......... that I should boast,..........
3. See, from His head,.......... His hands, His feet,..........

1. When I sur-vey the wond-rous cross,

On which the Prince.......... of glo-ry died,..........
Save in the death.......... of Christ, my Lord;..........
Sor-row and love.......... flow min-gled down;..........

On which the Prince of glo-ry died,

My rich-est gain.......... I count but loss,..........
All earth-ly things.......... that charm me most,..........
Did e'er such love.......... and sor-row meet,..........

My rich-est gain I count but loss,

And pour con-tempt.......... on all my pride.
I sac-ri-fice.......... them to His blood.
Or thorns com-pose.......... so rich a crown?

And pour con-tempt

122

The Wondrous Cross—Concluded.

Chorus.

O wondrous cross where Je - sus died, And for my sins was cru - ci - fied;

My long-ing eyes look up to Thee, Thou blesed Lamb of Cal - va - ry.

121   I'll Live for Thee.

R. E. HUDSON.   C. R. DUNBAR.

1. My life, my love I give to Thee, Thou Lamb of God, who died for me ;
2. I now be-lieve Thou dost receive, For Thou hast died that I might live;
3. O Thou who died on Cal - va - ry, To save my soul and make me free;

CHO.—*I'll live for Thee, I'll live for Thee, And O how glad my soul should be,*

D. C. for CHO.

O may I ev - er faith - ful be, My Sav - iour and my God!
And now henceforth I'll trust in Thee, My Sav - iour and my God!
I con - se - crate my life to Thee, My Sav - iour and my God!
That Thou didst give Thy - self for me, My Sav - iour and my God!

Nothing to Pay!

F. R. H.   FRANCES R. HAVERGAL, by per.

1. Nothing to pay! ah, nothing to pay! Nev-er a word of ex-cuse to say!
2. Nothing to pay! the debt is so great; What will you do with the awful weight?
3. Nothing to pay! yes, nothing to pay! Je-sus has clear'd all the debt a-way,

Year af-ter year thou hast fill'd the score, Ow-ing thy Lord still more and more.
How shall the way of es-cape be made? Nothing to pay! yet it must be paid!
Blot-ted it out with His bleeding hand! Free and forgiven and lov'd you stand.

Hear the voice of Je - sus say, "Ver-i-ly thou hast no-thing to pay!
Hear the voice of Je - sus say, "Ver-i-ly thou hast no-thing to pay!
Hear the voice of Je - sus say, "Ver-i-ly thou hast no-thing to pay!

Ru - in'd, lost art thou, and yet I for-gave thee all thy debt!"
All has been put to My ac-count, I have paid the full a-mount."
Paid is the debt and the debt-or free! Now I ask thee Lovest thou Me?"

Nothing to Pay!—Concluded.

Chorus.

Noth-ing, noth-ing noth-ing to pay! Hear the voice of Je - sus say:

"Ruin ed, lost art thou, and yet I for - gave thee all thy debt!"

123   Come, let us Join.

Isaac Watts.   (BURLINGTON. C. M.)   J. F. Burrowes.

1. Come, let us join our cheer-ful songs, With angels round the throne;
2. "Wor-thy the Lamb that died," they cry, "To be ex - alt - ed thus!"
3. Je - sus is wor-thy to re - ceive Hon-or and pow'r di - vine;
4. The whole cre - a - tion join in one, To bless the sa - cred name

Ten thousand, thousand are their tongues, But all their joys are one.
"Wor - thy the Lamb," our lips reply," "For He was slain for us!"
And blessings, more than we can give, Be, Lord! for ev - er Thine.
Of Him, that sits up - on the throne, And to a - dore the Lamb.

123

We'll Wait and Watch.

H. L. Hastings, by per.

Geo. C. Stebbins.

1. There's a light that is shin-ing in dark-ness, While we wait for the
2. From the sure word the prophets have spok-en, There is light flash-ing
3. Now we sing 'mid the darkness and shadows, And we pray and we
4. We are not of the night nor of darkness, Let us walk, then, as

dawn-ing of day; And it cheers us a-long on our jour-ney,
forth thro' the gloom; For the Scrip-ture can nev-er be bro-ken,
watch for the dawn; Till the Day-star, in glo-ry a-ris-ing,
chil-dren of day; Our weep-ing shall be for a mo-ment,

Chorus.

Till the shad-ows shall van-ish a-way.
And the King in His glo-ry will come.
Shall be-tok-en the com-ing of morn.
And our joy shall ne'er van-ish a-way.

So we'll wait and

watch for the dawn-ing, The day of e-ter-ni-ty blest; Then

We'll Wait and Watch.—Concluded.

take the wings of the morn - ing, And fly a - way to our rest.

125 Happy Day.

P. DODDRIDGE. E. F. RIMBAULT.

1. { O hap-py day that fixed my choice On Thee, my Sav-iour and my God! }
   { Well may this glowing heart rejoice, And tell its rapt-ures all a - broad. }

S. CHORUS. FINE.

Hap - py day, hap - py day, When Je - sus washed my sins a - way;

D. S.

He taught me how to watch and pray, And live re - joic - ing ev -'ry day;

2 O happy bond, that seals my vows
   To Him who merits all my love;
   Let cheerful anthems fill His house,
   While to that sacred shrine I move.

3 'Tis done; the great transaction's done;
   I am my Lord's, and He is mine;
   He drew me, and I followed on,
   Charmed to confess the voice divine.

4 Now rest, my long-divided heart,
   Fix'd on this blissful centre, rest;
   Nor ever from thy Lord depart,
   With Him of every good possess'd.

5 High Heav'n, that heard the solemn vow,
   That vow renewed shall daily hear,
   Till in life's latest hour I bow,
   And bless in death a bond so dear.

127

126 O Blessed be the Name.

ADON. A. JUDSON.

IRA D. SANKEY.

1. My joy - ful heart is filled with praise di-vine, Bless-ed be the
2. For ev - ery gift His lov - ing hand be- stows, Bless-ed be the
3. 'Tis He that makes the path be - fore me bright, Bless-ed be the

name of the Lord; For I am His and He is ev - er mine,
name of the Lord; For peace that like a gen - tle riv - er flows,
name of the Lord; No cloud can veil His glo - ry from my sight,

Bless-ed be the name of the Lord; For me the weight of
Bless-ed be the name of the Lord; For grace that keeps me
Bless-ed be the name of the Lord; O wondrous love that

sin He bore, O bless-ed be the name of the Lord; He saves me
hour by hour, O bless-ed be the name of the Lord; For vic - t'ry
ransomed me, O bless-ed be the name of the Lord; I'll sing His

128

O Blessed be the Name.—Concluded.

now and saves me ev - er - more, Blessed be the name of the Lord.
o'er the cru - el tempter's pow'r, Blessed be the name of the Lord.
praise thro' all e - ter - ni - ty, Blessed be the name of the Lord.

127 We would see Jesus.

ANNA B. WARNER.

F. MENDELSSOHN, arr.

1. We would see Je - sus—for the shadows length-en A - cross this
2. We would see Je - sus—the great Rock-foun-da - tion, Where-on our
3. We would see Je - sus—oth - er lights are pal - ing, Which for long

lit - tle land-scape of our life; We would see Je - sus, our weak
feet were set with sov'reign grace; Not life, nor death, with all their
years we have re - joiced to see; The bless-ings of our pil - grim-

faith to strengthen For the last wea - ri - ness—the fi - nal strife.
ag - i - ta - tion, Can thence re-move us, if we see His face.
age are fail - ing; We would not mourn them, for we go to Thee.

129

128 Here Am I, Send Me.

Rev. Daniel March.   Ira D. Sankey.

1. Hark! the voice of Je - sus cry-ing—"Who will go   and work to-day?
2. If   you can - not cross the o - cean, And the hea - then lands ex-plore,
3. If   you can - not speak like an-gels, If   you can - not preach like Paul,

Fields are white and har-vest   wait-ing; Who will bear the sheaves a-way?"
You   can find   the hea-then   near-er,   You can help them at your   door.
You   can tell   the love of Je - sus, You can say He died for   all.

Loud and strong the Mas-ter call - eth, Rich re - ward He of - fers thee;
If   you can - not give your thousands, You can give   the wid-ow's mite;
If   you can - not rouse the wick - ed With the judgment's dread a-larms,

Rit.

Who will an-swer, glad-ly say-ing, "Here I   am; send me, send me!"
And the   least you do   for Je - sus, Will be pre - cious in   His sight.
You can   lead the lit - tle chil-dren To   the Sav - iour's waiting arms.

Here Am I, Send Me.—Concluded.

4 If you cannot be the watchman,
  Standing high on Zion's wall,
  Pointing out the path to heaven,
  Offering life and peace to all; [ties
  With your prayers and with your boun-
  You can do what heaven demands;
  You can be like faithful Aaron,
  Holding up the Prophet's hands.

5 Let none hear you idly saying,
  "There is nothing I can do,"
  While the souls of men are dying,
  And the Master calls for you.
  Take the task He gives you gladly,
  Let His work your pleasure be;
  Answer quickly when He calleth,
  "Here am I; send me, send me!"

129   Over the Ocean Wave.

JULIA W. SAMPSON.   WM. B. BRADBURY.

1. O - ver the o - cean wave, far, far a - way, There the poor
2. Here in this hap - py land we have the light Shin - ing from
3. Then, while the mis - sion ships glad ti - dings bring, List! as that

CHO.—Pit - y them, pit - y them, Christians at home, Haste with the

hea - then live, wait - ing for day; Grop-ing in ig - norance,
God's own word, free, pure, and bright; Shall we not send to them
hea - then band joy - ful - ly sing, "O - ver the o - cean wave,
Bread of Life, hast - en and come.

dark as the night, No blessed Bi - ble to give them the light.
Bi - bles to read, Teachers, and preachers, and all that they need?
oh, see them come, Bringing the Bread of Life, guid-ing us home."

By per. The Biglow & Main Co.

130 Watch and Pray.

A.

JAMES McGRANAHAN.

1. Watch and pray! when Satan tempts thee, When assail'd by foes unseen;
2. Watch! for Satan's hosts surround thee, Gird thine armor on each day;
3. Pray! for thou art weak and helpless, Poor and wretched and undone;

Christ is ever near to shield thee; In thy conflicts look to Him.
They are waiting to ensnare thee; Look to Jesus, watch and pray.
None can face the pow'rs of darkness, Save in strength of Christ alone.

Chorus.

Watch and pray,...... the time is pass - ing, ... Sin and

Watch and pray, the time is pass-ing,

strife...... will soon be o'er: Watch and pray......

Sin and strife will soon be o'er: Watch and pray

Watch and Pray.—Concluded.

till Glo-ry's dawn-ing—Then we'll praise .... for ev-er-more.

131   Jesus, Saviour, Pilot Me.

Rev. Edward Hopper.   J. E. Gould.

1. Je - sus, Sav - iour, pi - lot me,   O - ver life's tem-pest-uous sea;
2. As a moth - er stills her child,   Thou canst hush the o-cean wild;
3. When at last I near the shore,   And the fear - ful breakers roar

Unknown waves be - fore me roll,   Hid - ing rock and treach'rous shoal;
Boist'rous waves o - bey Thy will,   When Thou say'st to them "Be still!"
'Twixt me and the peace - ful rest,   Then, while lean-ing on Thy breast,

Chart and com - pass come from Thee: Je - sus, Sav - iour, pi - lot me.
Wondrous Sov'reign of the sea,   Je - sus, Sav - iour, pi - lot me.
May I hear Thee say to me,   "Fear not, I will pi - lot thee."

132 Marching Through the World.

F. J. CROSBY.   IRA D. SANKEY.

1. We are marching thro' the world with our col - ors now un-furled,
2. We are marching on - ward still His commandments to ful - fill;
3. We are marching day by day, in the strait and nar-row way;

And to - geth - er we will sing the hap - py cho - rus;
And to la - bor for His king - dom—our en - deav - or;
Tell - ing out the joy - ful ti - dings of sal - va - tion;

While we hast-en to the strife on the bat - tle - field of life,
Press-ing on-ward at His call, we shall nev - er, nev - er fall,
This the mes-sage we pro-claim in our blest Re-deem-er's name,

With the Sav - iour's roy - al ban - ner float - ing o'er us.
But be vic - tor's thro' our Lead - er now and ev - er.
"There is par - don full and free for ev - ery na - tion."

13-1

Marching Thro' the World.—Concluded.

Chorus.

Keep step,   keep step,

We are march-ing, we are marching, Ev-er joy-ful as we

Keep step,   keep step,

Keep step,

go;   And the song we glad-ly sing is of Christ our com-ing

Keep step,

King, While His roy-al ban-ner still is wav-ing o'er us.

4 We are marching through the world, may our colors ne'er be furled,
   But with courage and with vigor be defended;
  Till we hear the joyful cry, that shall echo by and by,
  "We have conquered and the battle now is ended."
     Cho.—We are marching, etc.

135

133   Jesus, Lover of my Soul.

C. WESLEY.   (May be sung to MARTYN, No. 142.)   THEO. E. PERKINS.

1. Je - sus, Lov - er of my soul, Let me to Thy bo - som fly,
2. Oth - er ref - uge have I none, Hangs my help - less soul on Thee;
3. Thou, O Christ, art all I want; More than all in Thee I find:

While the near - er wa - ters roll, While the temp - est still is high;
Leave, oh, leave me not a - lone, Still sup - port and com - fort me.
Raise the fall - en, cheer the faint, Heal the sick, and lead the blind.

Hide me, oh, my Sav - iour, hide, Till the storm of life is past;
All my trust on Thee is stay'd, All my help from Thee I bring;
Just and ho - ly is Thy name, I am all un - right - eous - ness;

Safe in - to the ha - ven guide, Oh, re - ceive my soul at last.
Cov - er my de - fence - less head With the shad - ow of Thy wing.
Vile, and full of sin I am, Thou art full of truth and grace.

136

The Homeland.

134

Rev. H. R. Haweis.

Geo. C. Stebbins.

1. The Home-land! Oh! the Home-land! The land of the free-born!
2. My Lord is in the Home-land, With an gels bright and fair;
3. My loved ones in the Home-land Are wait-ing me to come

There's no night in the Home-land, But aye the fade-less morn:
There's no sin in the Home-land, And no temp-ta-tion there;
Where nei ther death nor sor row In-vade their ho ly home:

I'm sigh-ing for the Home-land, My heart is ach-ing here;
The mu-sic of the Home-land Is ring-ing in my ears;
O dear, dear na-tive Coun-try! O rest and peace a-bove!

There is no pain in the Home-land To which I'm draw ing near,
And when I think of the Home-land My eyes are filled with tears;
Christ bring us all to the Home-land Of Thine e-ter-nal love;

There is no pain in the Home-land To which I'm draw-ing near.
And when I think of the Home-land My eyes are filled with tears!
Christ bring us all to the Home-land Of Thine e-ter-nal love!

137

135 Our Fatherland.

F. J. CROSBY.   JNO. R. SWENEY.

1. Our Fa - ther-land,.. thy name so   dear,.. Our souls re - peat while strangers here;
2. A - bove the stars,.. a-bove the skies,.. Thy tow'ring hills.. in beau-ty rise;
3. There Je-sus reigns,.. our Saviour-King,.. And one by   one... His own will bring
4. No tears shall dim,.. no pain de - stroy... The light of peace, the smile of joy;

And oh, how   oft ... we sigh for thee... Dear Father-land,.. be-yond the   sea.
Where sunny fields. with ver-dure glow, And fadeless flow'rs in beau-ty   grow.
Thy songs to join,.. thy bliss to   share, O   Father - land,.. O Zi - on fair.
No more we'll clasp the part-ing hand With-in thy gates, our Fa - ther-land.

Chorus.

Our Fa - ther - land,.......... dear Fa - ther - land,.......... We long to
Our Father-land,   dear Father-land,

press.......... thy golden strand.......... And hail the bright........ and shining
We long to press, we long to press thy golden strand,   And hail the bright

Our Fatherland.—Concluded.

band,.......... In thy sweet vales,.......... dear Fa - ther-land......

and shining band, In thy sweet vales, dear Father-land.

136   Praise Him! Praise Him!

F. J. CROSBY.   CHESTER G. ALLEN.

1. Praise Him! praise Him! Je-sus, our bless-ed Re-deem - er! Sing, O earth—His
2. Praise Him! praise Him! Je-sus, our bless-ed Re-deem - er! For our sins He
3. Praise Him! praise Him! Je-sus, our bless-ed Re-deem - er! Heav'n-ly por - tals

won - der - ful love pro - claim!   Hail Him! hail Him! high-est arch-an - gels in
suf-fered, and bled, and died;   He our Rock, our hope of e - ter - nal sal-
loud with ho - san - nas ring!   Je - sus, Sav - iour, reign-eth for ev - er and
D S—*Praise Him! praise Him! tell of His ex - cel - lent*

glo - ry; Strength and hon-or give to His ho - ly name!   Like a shep-herd,
va - tion, Hail Him! hail Him! Je - sus, the Cru - ci - fied.   Sound His prais - es!
ev - er; Crown Him! crown Him! Prophet, and Priest, and King! Christ is com - ing!
greatness, Praise Him! praise Him! ever in joy - ful song!

D S.

Je-sus will guard His children, In His arms He car-ries them all day long;
Je-sus who bore our sor-rows, Love un - bound-ed, won-der - ful, deep, and strong;
o - ver the world vic - to-rious, Pow'r and glo - ry un - to the Lord be - long;

139

137 Lead Me, Saviour

F. M. D.

FRANK M. DAVIS.

1 Sav - iour, lead me, lest I stray (lest I stray), Gen - tly
2 Thou the ref - uge of my soul (of my soul) When life's
3 Sav - iour, lead me, till at last (till at last), When the

1 Sav - iour, lead me, lest I stray, Gen -

lead me all the way (all the way); I am safe when by Thy
storm - y bil - lows roll (bil - lows roll), I am safe when Thou art
storm of life is past (life is past), I shall reach the land of

tly lead me all the way; I am

side (by Thy side), I would in Thy love a - bide (love a - bide).
nigh (Thou art nigh), On Thy mer - cy I re - ly (I re - ly).
day (land of day), Where all tears are wip'd a - way (wip'd a way).

safe when by Thy side, I would in Thy love a - bide.

Chorus.

Lead me, lead me, Sav - iour, lead me, lest I stray;..........

Sav - iour, lead me, lest I stray;

rit. e dim.

Gen - tly down the stream of time, Lead me, Saviour, all the way (all the way).

stream of time, all the way,

144

138   Tell the Glad Story Again.

JULIA STERLING.

IRA D. SANKEY.

1. Tell the glad sto - ry of Je - sus who came, Full of com pass - ion, the
2. Tell the glad sto - ry where, sad and oppress'd, Ma - ny in bond - age are
3. Tell the glad sto - ry with pa-tience and love, Urg - ing the lost ones His
4. Tell the glad sto - ry when Jordan's dark wave Call - eth our loved ones its

lost to re - claim; Tell of re - demp - tion thro' faith in His name;
sigh - ing for rest; Tell them in Je - sus they all may be blest;
mer - cy to prove; Tell them of man - sions pre - par - ing a - bove;
bil - lows to brave; Tell them that Je - sus is Might-y to save;

Refrain.

Tell the glad sto - ry a - gain.
Tell the glad sto - ry a - gain.
Tell the glad sto - ry a - gain.
Tell the glad sto - ry a - gain.

Tell............... it a -

Tell it a - gain,

gain,............... Tell............... it a gain...............

tell it a - gain, Tell it a - gain, Tell it a - gain,

Tell the glad sto - ry to suf - fer - ing man; Tell it O tell it a - gain.

139   The Banner of the Cross.

El Nathan.   James McGranahan.

1. There's a royal banner giv-en for dis-play To the sol-diers
2. Tho' the foe may rage and gath-er as the flood, Let the stan-dard
3. O-ver land and sea, wher-ev-er man may dwell, Make the glo-rious
4. When the glo-ry dawns—'tis dawn-ing ver-y near—It is hast'ning

of the King; As an en-sign fair we lift it up to-day,
be dis-played; And be-neath its folds, as sol-diers of the Lord,
ti-dings known; Of the crim-son ban-ner now the sto-ry tell,
day by day— Then be-fore our King the foe shall dis-ap-pear.

Chorus.

While as ran-somed ones we sing.
For the truth be not dis-mayed!
While the Lord shall claim His own!
And the Cross the world shall sway.

March-ing on!........ March-ing
March-ing on! on! on! March-ing

on!......... For Christ count ev-ery thing but loss;........... And to
on! on! on! For Christ count ev-ery thing, ev-ery-thing but loss; And to

crown Him King, toil and sing, 'Neath the ban-ner of the cross.
crown Him King, we'll toil and sing, Be-neath the ban-ner of the cross

Copyright, 1884 & 1887, by James McGranahan. Used by per.

142

140 Sound the Battle-Cry!

WM. F. SHERWIN.   WM. F. SHERWIN.

Vigorously, in march time.

1. Sound the bat - tle cry! See! the foe is nigh; Raise the stand - ard high
2. Strong to meet the foe, Marching on we go, While our cause we know
3. Oh! Thou God of all, Hear us when we call Help us one and all

For the Lord; Gird your ar - mor on, Stand firm ev - ery one; Rest your
Must pre vail; Shield and ban - ner bright, Gleam - ing in the light; But thing
By Thy grace; When the bat - tle's done, And the vic t'ry won, May we

Chorus. *ff*

cause up on His ho - ly word }
for the right We ne'er can fail. } Rouse then, sol - diers! ral - ly round the
wear the crown Be - fore Thy face. }

ban ner. Read - y, stead - y, pass the word a - long; On - ward for - ward,

shout a - loud Ho - san - nah! Christ is Cap-tain of the might - y throng.

141 Sowing the Precious Seed.

W. A. O.

W. A. OGDEN.

1. Sow - ing the pre - cious seed In the ear - ly dawn of morn - ing.
2. Sow - ing the pre - cious seed While the day is fast de - clin - ing.
3. Sow - ing the pre - cious seed With an ear - nest, true en - deav - or,

Sow-ing the pre-cious seed In the noon-day fair; Sow-ing the pre-cious seed,
Sow-ing the pre-cious seed In the twi-light dim; Sow-ing the pre-cious seed,
Sow-ing the pre-cious seed Of the gold-en grain; Sow-ing the pre-cious seed;

D. S.—*Break-ing the bread of life,*

For the youth-ful heart's a - dorn - ing. Sow - ing the pre - cious seed
Nei - ther doubt-ing, nor re - pin - ing, Leav - ing it all to God,
And the hand with-hold-ing nev - er, Pray - ing that God will send
Tell - ing o'er the gos - pel sto - ry, Sow ing the pre cious seed

Chorus.

FINE.

With a ten - der care.
Trust-ing all to Him. } Sow - ing the pre - cious seed, Sow - ing the
It the sun and rain.
For the dear home land.

We are

D. S.

pre - cious seed, Scat - ter - ing far and wide with pa - tient, lov - ing hand;

1-1-1.

142

Sinners, Turn.

C. WESLEY.   (MARTYN. 7s. D.)   S. B. MARSH.

FINE.

1. { Sin - ners, turn, why will ye die! God, your Mak - er, asks you— Why? }
   { God, who did your be - ing give, Made you with Him-self to live; }

D.C.— Why, ye thank-less crea-tures, why Will ye cross His love, and die?

He the fa - tal cause de mands, Asks the work of His own hands,—

D. C.

2 Sinners, turn, why will ye die?
God, your Saviour, asks you—Why?
He who did your souls retrieve,
Died Himself that ye might live.
Will ye let Him die in vain?
Crucify your Lord again?
Why, ye ransomed sinners, why
Will ye slight His grace, and die?

3 Sinners, turn, why will ye die!
God, the Spirit, asks you—Why?
He, who all your lives hath strove,
Urged you to embrace His love:
Will ye not His grace receive?
Will ye still refuse to live?
Why, ye long-sought sinners! why,
Will ye grieve your God, and die?

143

How Sweet the Name.

JOHN NEWTON.   (EVAN. C. M.)   W. H. HAVERGAL.

1. How sweet the name of Je - sus sounds In a be - liev - er's ear;
2. It makes the wound - ed spir - it whole, And calms the troub - led breast;
3. Dear Name the Rock on which I build, My shield and hid - ing - place;
4. Je - sus, my Shep - herd, Sav-iour, Friend, My Pro-phet, Priest and King;
5. I would Thy bound - less love pro - claim With ev - ery fleet - ing breath;

It soothes his sor - rows, heals his wounds, And drives a - way his fear.
'Tis man - na to the hun - gry soul, And to the wea - ry, rest.
My nev - er - fail - ing treas-ure, filled With bound-less stores of grace.
My Lord, my Life, my Way, my End.— Ac - cept the praise I bring.
So shall the mu - sic of Thy name Re - fresh my soul in death.

145

144 When the Mists have Rolled Away.

ANNIE HERBERT, arr.

IRA D. SANKEY.

1. When the mists have rolled in splen-dor From the beau-ty of the hills,
2. Oft we tread the path be-fore us With a wea-ry burden'd heart;
3. We shall come with joy and glad-ness, We shall gath-er round the throne;

And the sun-light falls in glad-ness On the riv-er and the rills,
Oft we toil a-mid the shad-ows, And our fields are far a-part;
Face to face with those that love us, We shall know as we are known;

We re-call our Fa-ther's prom-ise In the rain-bow of the spray.
But the Sav-iour's "Come, ye bless-ed," All our la-bor will re-pay,
And the song of our re-demp-tion, Shall re-sound thro' end-less day,

rit.

We shall know each oth-er bet-ter When the mists have rolled a-way.
When we gath-er in the morn-ing Where the mists have rolled a-way.
When the shad-ows have de-part-ed, And the mists have rolled a-way.

Chorus.

We shall know.......... as we are known,.......... Nev-er-
as we are known,
as we are known,

We shall know as we are known,

When the Mists.—Concluded.

more............ to walk a - lone,.... .... In the

Nev - er - more to walk a - lone, to walk a - lone,

dawn - ing of the morn - ing Of that bright and hap py day:

We shall know each oth - er bet - ter, When the mists have rolled a - way.

145   Take My Life, and let it Be.

F. R. HAVERGAL, by per.   W. A. MOZART arr by H. P. MAIN.

1. Take my life and let it be Con se crat ed, Lord, to Thee;
2. Take my feet and let them be Swift and beau ti ful for Thee;
3. Take my mo ments and my days, Let them flow in end less praise;
4. Take my will and make it Thine, It shall be no lon ger mine;
5. Take my love, my God I pour At Thy feet its treas ure store;

Take my hands and let them move At the im pulse of Thy love,
Take my voice and let me sing At ways—on ly for my King,
Take my in tel lect, and use Ev ry pow'r as Thou shalt choose,
Take my heart, it is Thine own, It shall be Thy roy al throne.
Take my self, and I will be Ev - er, on - ly, all for Thee.

Rock of Ages.

A. M. TOPLADY.   E. O. EXCELL.
Soprano prominent.

1. Rock... ...... of A - - - ges, cleft ... . for me,
2. Could........ . my tears........... for ev - - er flow.
3. While........ I draw........... this fleet - - ing breath,

1. Rock of A - ges, cleft for me, Blest Rock of A - ges, cleft for me,
2. Could my tears for ev - er flow. Oh, could my tears for ev - er flow.
3. While I draw this fleet-ing breath, Yes, while I draw this fleet-ing breath,

Let............ me hide .... my - self .... in Thee;
Could .... my zeal .... no lan - - guor know–
When .... my eyes........... shall close........ in death,

Let me hide my - self in Thee Oh let me hide my - self in Thee,
Could my zeal no tan - guor know Oh, could my zeal no languor know–
When my eyes shall close in death, Yes, when my eyes shall close in death,

Let ... . the wa - - - ter and........... the blood,
These .... for sin .... could not .... a - tone.
When .... I rise........... to worlds ..... un - known,

Let the wa - ter and the blood, Oh, let the wa - ter and the blood,
These for sin could not a - tone. No, these for sin could not a - tone,
When I rise to worlds un-known, Yes, when I rise to worlds un-known,

Rock of Ages.—Concluded.

From .... Thy wound - - ed side.......... which flow'd,
Thou .... must save,......... and Thou .... a - lone;
And .... be - hold .... Thee on .... Thy throne—

From Thy wound-ed side which flow'd, Yes, from Thy wound ed side which flow'd,
Thou must save, and Thou a - lone, Yes, Thou must save, and Thou a - lone;
And be - hold Thee on Thy throne, Yes, and be - hold Thee on Thy throne—

rit.

Be .... of sin .... the doub - - le cure, ..
In .... my hand .... no price .... I bring,
Rock .... of A - - ges, cleft .... for me, ...

rit.

Be of sin the doub le cure, Yes, be of sin the doub le cure,
In my hand no price I bring, Lord, in my hand, no price I bring,
Rock of A - ges, cleft for me, Blest Rock of A - ges, cleft for me,

Repeat pp.

Save .... me from .... its guilt .... and pow'r.
Sim - - ply to .... Thy cross .... I cling.
Let .... me hide .... my - self .... in Thee.

Repeat pp

Save me from its guilt and pow'r, Yes, save me from its guilt and pow'r.
Sim - ply to Thy cross I cling, Lord, simp ly to Thy cross I cling.
Let me hide my - self in Thee, Oh, let me hide my - self in Thee.

149

147 Coming.

Rev. W. O. Cushing.

Ira D. Sankey.

1. O watchman on the mountain height, Proclaim the com - ing day; Be -
2. O watchman, bid the sleeping Church A - wake, a - rise and pray; The
3. All hail to Zi - on's glo - rious King, By proph-ets long fore - told; Praise

Chorus.

hold the spires of gold - en fires Point up-ward far a - way.
heav'nly Bridegroom soon will come, And now is on His way.
Him in song, ye an - gel throng, Strike all your harps of gold.
} Coming, yes, He's

com - ing, The Day-Spring from on high; Com-ing, yes, He's com - ing; The

prom-ised hour is nigh; Com-ing, yes, He's com - ing; Let all the ransomed

sing; The hills are bright with shining light; All hail the Com - ing King.

150

148   Blessed Assurance.

F. J. CROSBY.   MRS. JOSEPH F. KNAPP.

1. Bless - ed as - sur - ance, Je - sus is mine! O, what a fore - taste of
2. Per - fect sub - mis - sion, per - fect de - light, Vis - ions of rapt - ure now
3. Per - fect sub - mis - sion, all is at rest, I in my Sav - iour am

glo - ry di - vine! Heir of sal - va - tion, pur - chase of God,
burst on my sight, An - gels de - scend - ing bring from a - bove,
hap - py and blest, Watching and wait - ing, look - ing a - bove,

Chorus.

Born of His Spir - it, wash'd in His blood.
Ech - oes of mer - cy, whis-pers of love. } This is my sto - ry,
Filled with His good - ness, lost in His love.

this is my song, Prais-ing my Sav - iour all the day long; This is my

sto - ry, this is my song, Prais - ing my Sav - iour all the day long.

149 God will take Care of You.

F. J. CROSBY.

IRA D. SANKEY.

1. God will take care of you, be not a-fraid; He is your
2. God will take care of you thro' all the day, Shielding your
3. God will take care of you, long as you live, Granting you

safe - guard thro' sun - shine and shade; Ten - der - ly watch-ing and
foot - steps, di - rect - ing your way; He is your Shep-herd, Pro-
bless - ings no oth - er can give; He will take care of you

keep - ing His own, He will not leave you to wan - der a - lone.
teet - or and Guide, Lead-ing His chil - dren where still wa - ters glide.
when time is past, Safe to His king-dom will bring you at last.

Chorus.

God will take care of you still to the end; Oh, what a

Fa - ther, Re - deem - er and Friend! Je - sus will an - swer when-

God will take Care of You.—Concluded.

ev - er you call, He will take care of you, trust Him for all.

150   Sometime We'll Understand.

MAXWELL N. CORNELIUS, D.D.   JAMES McGRANAHAN.

1. Not now, but in the com-ing years, It may be in the bet-ter land,
2. We'll catch the broken threads a-gain, And fin - ish what we here be - gun;
3. We'll know why clouds instead of sun Were o - ver many a cher-ish'd plan;
4. Why what we long for most of all, E - ludes so oft our ea - ger hand;
5. God knows the way, He holds the key, He guides us with un-err-ing hand;

We'll read the mean-ing of our tears, And there, sometime, we'll un-der-stand.
Heav'n will the mys-ter-ies ex-plain, And then, ah, then, we'll un-der-stand.
Why song has ceased when scarce begun; 'Tis there, sometime we'll un-der-stand.
Why hopes are crush'd and cas-tles fall, Up there, sometime, we'll un-der-stand.
Some time with tear-less eyes we'll see; Yes, there, up there, we'll un-der-stand.

Chorus. *A little faster.*   doth hold thy hand;

doth hold thy hand;

Then trust in God thro' all thy days; Fear not, for He doth hold thy hand;

a tempo primo.   *cres.*   *ad lib.*

Tho' dark thy way, still sing and praise; Sometime, sometime, we'll un - der-stand.

Faith is the Victory.

JOHN H. YATES.   IRA D. SANKEY.

1. En-camped a - long the hills of light, Ye Chris - tian sol - diers, rise,
2. His ban - ner o - ver us is love, Our sword the word of God;
3. On ev - ery hand the foe we find Drawn up in dread ar - ray;
4. To Him that o - ver-comes the foe, White rai - ment shall be giv'n;

And press the bat - tle ere the night Shall veil the glow - ing skies;
We tread the road the saints a - bove With shouts of tri - umph trod;
Let tents of ease be left be - hind, And on - ward to the fray;
Be - fore the an - gels he shall know His name con - fessed in heaven;

A - gainst the foe in vales be - low, Let all our strength be hurled;
By faith they, like a whirlwind's breath, Swept on o'er ev - ery field;
Sal - va - tion's hel - met on each head, With truth all girt a - bout,
Then on - ward from the hills of light, Our hearts with love a - flame;

Faith is the vic - to - ry, we know, That o - ver-comes the world.
The faith by which they con-quered Death Is still our shin - ing shield.
The earth shall trem - ble 'neath our tread, And ech - o with our shout.
We'll van - quish all the hosts of night, In Je - sus' con-qu'ring name.

Chorus.

Faith is the vic - to - ry! Faith is the vic - to - ry!
Faith is   Faith is

Faith is the Victory.—Concluded.

Oh, glo - ri - ous vic - to - ry, That o - ver - comes the world.

152   Gird on the Royal Armor.

GRACE J. FRANCES.   HUBERT P. MAIN.

1. Gird on the roy - al ar - mor, Go forth in Je - sus' name;
2. Lift up the roy - al stand - ard, Go forth our cause to win,
3. With right-eous-ness our breast-plate, The Spir - it's sword in hand,

To those who sit in dark - ness The Light of Life pro - claim.
With hel - met, shield, and buck - ler, A - gainst the hosts of sin.
Still con - q'ring and to con - quer, Press on at God's com - mand.

Gird on the roy - al ar - mor, That we the foe may face;

And trust - ing our Com - mand - er, Be vic - tors thro' His grace.

Thy Light is Come.

M. E. SERVOSS.

H. R. PALMER.

Duet. *Not too fast.*

1. Give thanks un - to God who is a - ble and will-ing To save to the
2. Sweet Hope in the home of the drunk-ard hath ris - en, Where the darkness of
3. Then ban - ish the wine - cup, and seek for a bless-ing From Him in whose

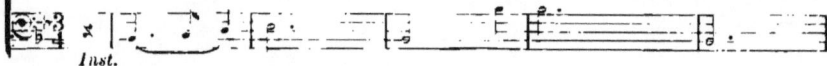

Inst.

ut - ter - most all who draw near; To send out His light, their re -
sor - row too long held its reign; He hath cast off his fet - ters, and
might you a - lone can pre - vail; For they who will seek Him, their

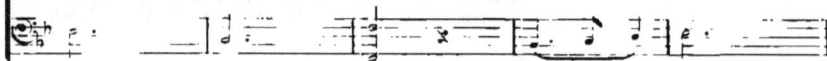

demp - tion ful - fill - ing, While His won - der ful love shall dis - pel ev - er - y fear.
burst from his pris - on, And the sun - shine of joy fills his heart once a - gain.
weak ness con - fess - ing, Shall have strength to re - sist all the foes who as - sail.

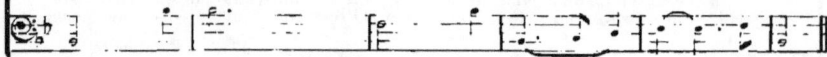

Chorus. *Spirited.*

A - rise! a - rise! A - rise, for thy light is come!
A - rise! a - rise!

A - rise! a - rise! A - rise, for thy light is come!
A - rise, a - rise!

Thy Light is Come.—Concluded.

The light.......... of truth .... To lead.......... thee
The light of His truth and love, To lead to thy

home;
home a-bove; A-rise! oh! a-rise, for thy light is come!

---

154   Glory to His Name.

Rev. E. A. HOFFMAN.   Rev. J. H STOCKTON, by per.

1. Down at the cross where my Sav-iour died, Down, where for cleans-ing from
2. I am so wondrous-ly sav'd from sin, Je-sus so sweet-ly a
3. Oh, pre-cious fount-ain that saves from sin, I am so glad I have
4. Come to this fount-ain, so rich and sweet; Cast thy poor soul at the

sin I cried; There to my heart was the blood ap-plied; Glo-ry to His
bides with-in; There at the cross where He took me in, Glo-ry to His
en-ter'd in; There Je-sus saves me and keeps me clean, Glo-ry to His
Sav-iour's feet; Plunge in to-day, and be made com-plete; Glo-ry to His

FINE. Chorus.   D. S.

name. Glo-ry to His name,.... Glo-ry to His name....

157

155 Revive Us Again.

Rev. W. P. MACKAY.   JOHN J. HUSBAND.

1. We praise Thee, O God! for the Son of Thy love, For.... Je-sus who
2. We praise Thee, O God! for Thy Spir-it of light, Who has shown us our
3. All glo-ry and praise to the Lamb that was slain, Who has borne all our
4. All glo-ry and praise to the God of all grace, Who has bought us, and
5. Re-vive us a-gain; fill each heart with Thy love; May each soul be re-

Chorus.

died, and is now gone a-bove.
Sav-iour, and scat-tered our night.
sins, and has cleansed ev-ery stain. } Hal-le-lu-jah! Thine the glo-ry, Hal-le-
sought us, and guid-ed our ways.
kin-dled with fire from a-bove.

lu-jah! A-men; Hal-le-lu-jah! Thine the glo-ry, Re-vive us a-gain.

156 (TEMPERANCE.) To the Rescue. (Tune above.)

1 A foe is abroad, like a tyrant he reigns,
  And his captives are groaning in fetters and chains.

CHO:— { To the rescue, let us hasten; to the rescue,—away!
        { To the rescue of the fallen, O hasten to day.

2 With faith in the Lord and the pow'r of His might,
  Let the armies of temp'rance their forces unite.

3 Go tell of God's love, and the demon shall fall;
  Go tell them of Jesus, the Saviour of all.

4 Go seek out the lost in their bondage of sin,
  There's hope for the fallen, go gather them in.

Copyright, 1894, by The Biglow & Main Co.   F. J. CROSBY.

157 Blest be the Tie.

Rev. JOHN FAWCETT.   (DENNIS. S. M.)   H. G. NAGELI.

1. Blest be the tie that binds Our hearts in Chris-tian love;
2. Be-fore our Fa-ther's throne, We pour our ar-dent pray'rs;

158

Blest be the Tie.—Concluded.

The fel - low - ship of kin - dred minds Is like to that a - bove.
Our fears, our hopes, our aims are one,— Our com - forts and our cares.

3 We share our mutual woes;
  Our mutual burdens bear;
  And often for each other flows
  The sympathizing tear.

4 When we asunder part,
  It gives us inward pain;
  But we shall still be join'd in heart,
  And hope to meet again.

158   When Winds are Raging.

HARRIET B. STOWE.   JHAN A. DYKES.

1. When winds are rag - ing o'er the up - per o - cean, And bil - lows wild con -
2. Far, far be-neath, the noise of tempests di - eth, And sil - ver waves chime
3. So to the heart that knows Thy love, O Pur - est! There is a tem - ple,
4. Far, far a - way, the roar of pas - sion di - eth, And lov - ing tho'ts rise

tend with an - gry roar, 'Tis said, far down, be - neath the wild com -
ev - er peace-ful - ly, And no rude storm, how fierce so - e'er it
sa - cred ev - er - more, And all the bab - ble of life's an - gry
calm and peace-ful - ly, And no rude storm, how fierce so - e'er it

mo - tion, That peace - ful still - ness reign - eth ev - er - more.
ti - eth, Dis - turbs the Sab - bath of that deep - er sea.
voic - es Dies in hushed still - ness at its peace - ful door.
ti - eth, Dis - turbs the soul that dwells, O Lord, in Thee.

159 True-Hearted, Whole-Hearted.

FRANCES R. HAVERGAL, by per.

GEO. C. STEBBINS.

1. True-heart-ed, whole-heart-ed, faith-ful and loy-al, King of our
2. True-heart-ed, whole-heart-ed, full-est al-le-giance Yield-ing hence-
3. True-heart-ed, whole-heart-ed, Sav-iour all glo-rious! Take Thy great

lives, by Thy grace we will be; Un-der the stan-dard ex-
forth to our glo-ri-ous King; Val-iant en-deav-or and
pow-er and reign there a-lone, O-ver our wills and af-

alt-ed and roy-al, Strong in Thy strength we will bat-tle for Thee.
lov-ing o-be-dience, Free-ly and joy-ous-ly now would we bring.
fec-tions vic-to-rious, Free-ly sur-ren-dered and whol-ly Thine own.

Chorus.

Peal out the watchword! si-lence it nev-er! Song of our
Peal si-lence Song

spir-its re-joic-ing and free; Peal out the watchword!
re-joic-ing Peal

True-Hearted, Whole-Hearted.—Concluded.

loy - al for - ev - or, King of our lives, By Thy grace we will be.

loy - al   King

·160   A Song for Water Bright.

GEO. COOPER.   IRA D. SANKEY.

1 A   song, a   song for   wa - ter bright, In   love and beau - ty flow - ing!
2 There's balm in   ev - ery   sparkling drop, In   ev - ery wave there's pleasure;
3 It   nerves the   hand to   deeds of might! It   wakes the heart to   glad - ness!
4 From ev - ery   vale and   glade and hill It   speaks of   na - ture's kind - ness!

It   sings its   way in   joy and might, The   gift of heav'n be - stow - ing.
In   dia mond spray it   leaps a   way, A   love ly   boon and   treas - ure;
It   breathes a psalm of   pure de light, And   charms us   all from sad - ness!
O,   may we heed the   les   son still, Nor   shun it   in our   blind ness!

Chorus.

A   song, a   song for   wa - ter fair; As   pure and free   as   mount-ain air;

A   song, a   song for wa - ter   fair, As   pure and   free as   mount-ain air.

161

161   I will Sing the Wondrous Story.

F. H. RAWLEY.

PETER BILHORN.

1. I will sing the won-drous sto - ry, Of the Christ who died for me,
2. I was lost, but Je - sus found me, Found the sheep that went a - stray;
3. I was bruised, but Je - sus healed me, Faint was I from many a fall,
4. Days of dark - ness still come o'er me, Sor - row's paths I oft - en tread,
5. He will keep me till the riv - er Rolls its wa - ters at my feet;

How He left His home in glo - ry, For the cross on Cal - va - ry.
Threw His lov - ing arms a - round me, Drew me back in - to His way.
Sight was gone, and fears pos-sessed me, But He freed me from them all.
But the Sav - iour still is with me, By His hand I'm safe - ly led.
Then He'll bear me safe - ly o - ver, Where the loved ones I shall meet.

Chorus.

Yes, I'll sing.......... the won-drous sto - - - - ry
Yes, I'll sing   the won-drous sto - ry

Of the Christ.......... who died for me, ...
Of the Christ   who died for me,

Sing it with.......... the saints in glo - - - - ry,
Sing it with   the saints in glo - ry,

162

I will Sing.—Concluded.

Gath - ered by.......... the crys - tal sea,

gath - ered by the crys - tal sea.

162   I am Trusting Thee, Lord Jesus.

FRANCES R. HAVERGAL, by per.   J. H. BURKE.

1. I am trust - ing Thee, Lord Je - sus   Trust - ing on - ly Thee!
2. I am trust - ing Thee for par - don,   At   Thy feet   I   bow:
3. I am trust - ing Thee for cleans - ing In   the crim - son flood;
4. I am trust - ing Thee for pow - er,   Thine can nev - er fail;
5. I am trust - ing Thee, Lord Je - sus,   Nev - er let   me   fall;

Trust - ing Thee for full sal - va - tion,   Great and free.
For Thy grace and ten - der mer - cy,   Trust - ing now.
Trust - ing Thee to make me ho - ly,   By Thy blood.
Words which Thou Thy - self shalt give me,   Must pre - vail.
I   am trust - ing Thee for ev - er,   And for all.

Chorus.

I   am   trust - ing,   Trust - ing on - ly Thee.
I am trust - ing, I am trust - ing,

I am trust - ing, trust - ing.   Trust - ing on - ly Thee.
trust - ing, trust - ing, I am trust - ing,

163

163 For Christ and the Church.

F. J. CROSBY.   [SECOND TUNE]   Rev. ROBERT LOWRY.

1. We gath-er a-gain in the name of our Lord, As hum-ble dis-
2. Our Christian En-deav-or—to hon-or His laws, To work for His
3. O Sav-iour, we ask Thee to grant us in love Thy Spir-it to

ci - ples to learn from His word; We look in its pa - ges true
glo - ry, be true to His cause; To vis - it the low - ly, the
teach us with light from a - bove; Re - vive all our mem-bers, give

wis - dom to know, And fol low our Sav - iour, wher-ev - er we go.
poor and op-press'd, And points them to Je - sus for ref - uge and rest.
strength to our bands, And pros - per, we pray Thee, the work of our hands.

Chorus.

For Christ and the Church! O hear the glad sound; For Christ and the Church!

Let our watch word re - sound; For "Christ and the Church!" By His

164

For Christic and the Church. —Concluded.

grace we will live, Our whole-heart-ed serv-ice To Him we will give.

164   Hide Me.

F. J. CROSBY.

W. H. DOANE.

1. Hide me, O my Sav-iour, hide me In Thy ho-ly place;
2. Hide me, when the storm is rag-ing O'er life's troub-led sea;
3. Hide me, when my heart is break-ing With its weight of woe;

Rest-ing there be-neath Thy glo-ry, O let me see Thy face.
Like a dove on o-cean's bil-lows, O let me fly to Thee.
When in tears I seek the com-fort Thou cans't a-lone be-stow.

Refrain.

Hide me, me hide, O bless-ed Sav-iour, hide me;
Hide me, hide me, safe-ly hide me,

O Sav-iour, keep me Safe-ly, O Lord, with Thee.
O, my Sav-iour, keep Thou me,

165   Army of Endeavor.

R. A. DYKES.

IRA D. SANKEY.

1. Ar - my of En - deav - or, hear the trum - pet call; 'Gainst the foe ad -
2. In His roy - al serv - ice there's a work for all, Cheer - ing on the
3. Ev - er press - ing on - ward in the cause of right, Hold - ing up the

vanc - ing, for - ward, one and all; Christ is our Com-mand - er;
faint ones, lift - ing those that fall; Un - to Him who calls us
ban - ner, walk - ing in the light; Keep - ing His com-mand - ments,

faith - ful let us be; He will give to us the vic - to - ry.
ev - er faith - ful be; He will give to us the vic - to - ry.
great re - ward have we; He will give to us the vic - to - ry.

Chorus.

Though the bat - tle ra - ges, what have we to fear? In the wild - est

con - flict,— He is ev - er near; Trust - ing in our Lead - er,

Copyright, 1891, by The Biglow & Main Co.

Army of Endeavor.—Concluded.

faith - ful let us be; He will give the vic - to - ry.

166   O Help Me Tell the Story.

EDWARD SHIRAS.   RIAN A. DYKES.

1. O help me tell the sto - ry   Of Christ my Lord and King,
2. He brought me out of bond - age,   He paid my debt of sin;
3. He left His home in glo - ry,   He laid His scep - ter down,
4. Be this my one En - deav - or,   To glo - ri - fy His name;

For of His bound - less mer - cy   My soul de - lights to sing.
The door of Life He o - pened,   That I might en - ter in.
And on the cross He suf - fered,   That I might wear a crown.
The sto - ry of Re - demp - tion,   To all the world pro - claim.

Chorus.

O help me tell the sto - ry,   Of Je - sus' bound - less love,....

Till, with the Church tri - umph - ant,   I sing His praise a - bove.

167 O Glad and Glorious Gospel.

M. Fraser.

James McGranahan.

1. 'Tis a true and faith-ful say-ing, Je-sus died for sin-ful men;
2. He has made a full a-tone-ment, Now His sav-ing work is done;
3. Still up-on His hands the nail-prints, And the scars up-on His brow,
4. But re-mem-ber this same Je-sus In the clouds will come a-gain,

Tho' we've told the sto-ry oft - en, We must tell it o'er a - gain.
He has sat-is-fied the Fa-ther, Who ac-cepts us in His Son.
Our Re-deem-er, Lord and Sav-iour In the glo-ry stand-eth now.
And with Him His blood-bought peo-ple Ev-er-more shall live a-gain.

Chorus.

O glad and glo-rious Gos-pel! With joy we now pro-claim......
we now pro-claim

A full and free sal-va-tion, Thro' faith in Je-sus' name.

168 Nearer, My God, to Thee.

Sarah F. Adams.

(BETHANY. 6, 4.)

Lowell Mason.

1. Near-er, my God, to Thee, Near-er to Thee; E'en tho' it be a cross
2. Tho', like a wan-der-er, The sun gone down, Dark-ness be o-ver me,
3. There let the way ap-pear, Steps un-to heaven; All that Thou send-est me,
4. Then with my wak-ing tho'ts, Bright with Thy praise, Out of my sto-ny griefs,
5. Or if, on joy-ful wing, Cleav-ing the sky, Sun, moon, and stars for-got,

D.S.—Near - er, my God, to Thee!

168

Nearer, My God, to Thee.—Concluded.

FINE   D.S.

That rais-eth me;	Still all my song shall be—Near - er, my God, to Thee!
My rest a stone,	Yet in my dreams I'd be Near - er, my God, to Thee!
In mer - cy given;	An - gels to beck - on me Near - er, my God, to Thee!
Beth - el I'll raise;	So by my woes to be Near - er, my God, to Thee!
Up - ward I fly;	Still all my song shall be Near - er, my God, to Thee!
Near - er to Thee!	

169   Hear Us, O Saviour.

CHARLES BRUCE.   IRA D. SANKEY.

1. Hear us, O Sav - iour, while we pray, Hum - bly our need con - fess - ing;
2. Know - ing Thy love, on Thee we call, Bold - ly Thy throne ad - dress - ing;
3. Trust - ing Thy word that can - not fail, Mas - ter, we claim Thy prom - ise;

Grant us the prom-ised show'rs to - day, Send them up - on us, O Lord.
Plead-ing that show'rs of grace may fall,—Send them up - on us, O Lord.
Oh, that our faith may now pre-vail,—Send us the showers, O Lord.

Refrain.

Send show'rs of bless - ing; Send show'rs re - fresh - ing;

Send us show'rs of bless - ing; Send them, Lord, we pray.

170 Our Christian Band.

LYMAN G. CUYLER.

IRA D. SANKEY.

1. With cheer - ful songs.............. and hymns of praise,..............
2. And while we meet.............. to - geth - er here,..............
3. O Thou, who art.............. the chil - dren's Friend!..........

1. With cheer-ful songs and hymns of praise,

Our grate - ful hearts.............. to Him we raise,..............
In bonds of love.............. and friend-ship dear,..............
Our steps di - rect,.............. our paths de - fend, ...

Our grate-ful hearts to Him we raise,

Who leads us on .... with gen - tle hand,..............
O may our prayers.............. like in - cense rise,,..............
And, by Thine own .... al - might - ty hand,..............

Who leads us on with gen - tle hand,

And crowns with love.............. our Chris - tian Band..............
To Him whose grace .... each need sup - plies,..............
Pro - tect and keep .... our Chris - tian Band..............

And crowns with love our Christian Band.

rit.

Chorus.

Then glad - ly let us stand, U - nit - ed heart and hand, The

Copyright, 1893, by The Biglow & Main Co.

170

Our Christian Band.—Concluded.

lost to gath-er in, From sor - row, pain and sin; Be

this our con-stant aim, To spread a - broad the name Of

Je - sus, our Re - deem - er, And His won - drous love pro - claim.

171   Book of Grace and Glory!

THOMAS MACKELLAR.   DR. L. MASON.

1. Book of grace! and book of glo - ry! Gift of God to age and youth,
2. Book of love! in ac - cents ten - der Speak-ing un - to such as we;
3. Book of hope! the spir - it sigh - ing, Sweet-est com-fort finds in Thee,

Wondrous is Thy sa - cred sto-ry, Bright, bright with truth! Bright, bright with truth!
May it lead us, Lord to ren - der All, all to Thee. All, all to Thee.
As it hears the Sav-iour cry - ing, "Come, come to Me!" "Come, come to Me!"

171

172 Go Ye into All the World.

G. M. J.   JAMES McGRANAHAN.

1. Far, far a - way in hea then darkness dwell-ing, Mill-ions of souls for
2. See o'er the world the o - pen doors in - vit - ing, Sol-diers of Christ, a-
3. "Why will ye die?" the voice of God is call - ing, "Why will ye die?" re-
4. God speed the day when those of ev - 'ry na - tion "Glo - ry to God" tri-

ev - er may be lost; Who, who will go, sal va - tion's sto ry tell - ing,
rise and en - ter in! Breth'ren, a - wake! our forc - es all u - nit - ing,
ech o in His Name; Je - sus hath died to save from death ap - pall - ing,
umph ant - ly shall sing; Ransomed, redeemed, re - joic - ing in sal - va - tion,

Chorus.

Look-ing to Je - sus, heeding not the cost?
Send forth the gos-pel, break the chains of sin.
Life and sal-va - tion therefore go pro-claim.
Shout "Hal le - lu - jah, for the Lord is King."

"All pow'r is giv - en un - to me,

All pow'r is giv - en un - to me; Go ye in - to all the world and

preach the gos - pel, And lo, I am with you al - way."

173   Sunshine in the Soul.

E. E. HEWITT.   JNO. R. SWENEY.

1. There's sunshine in my soul to - day, More glo - ri - ous and bright,
2. There's mu - sic in my soul to - day, A car - ol to my King,
3. There's springtime in my soul to - day, For when the Lord is near,
4. There's gladness in my soul to - day, And hope, and praise, and love;

Than glows in a - ny earth ly sky, For Je - sus is my light.
And Je - sus, list - en - ing, can hear The songs I can - not sing.
The dove of peace sings in my heart, The flow'rs of grace ap - pear.
For bless - ings which He gives me now, For joys laid up a - bove.

Refrain.

Oh, there's sun - - - - shine, bless - ed sun - - - - - shine,
sun - shine in my soul, bless - ed sun - shine in my soul,

When the peace - ful, hap - py mo - ments roll;
hap - py mo - ments roll;

When Je - sus shows His smil - ing face, There is sun - shine in my soul.

174   That Old, Old Story is True.

D. B. WATKINS.   E. O. EXCELL.

1. There's a won - der - ful sto - ry I heard long a - go, 'Tis
2. They.... told of a Sav - iour so love - ly and pure, That

call'd "The sweet sto - ry of old;".... I..... hear it so
came on the earth.... to dwell,... To... seek for His

oft - en, wher - ev - er I go,.... That same old sto - ry is
lost ones, and make them se - cure... From death and the pow - er of

told;.... And I've thought it was strange that so oft - en they'd tell
hell; ... That.. He was de - spis'd, and with thorns He was crown'd,

That.. sto - ry as if it were new;.... But I've found out the
On the cross was ex - tend - ed to view;... And.... O, what sweet

174

That Old, Old Story.—Concluded.

rea - son they loved it so well, That old, old sto - ry is true.
peace in my heart since I've found That old, old sto - ry is true.

Refrain.

That old, old sto - ry is true,........ That old, old
That old, old sto - ry is true, ... That old, old

It is true,

sto - ry is true;...... But I've found out the rea - son they
sto - ry is true;...... But.... O, what sweet peace in my

It is true,

loved it so well, That old, old sto - ry is true.....
heart since I've found That old, old sto - ry is true.....

3.
He arose and ascended to heaven, we're told,
 Triumphant o'er death and the grave; [hold,
And His loved ones in glory His face shall be-
 And hail Him the Mighty to save.
Where our kindred we'll meet, and we'll never-
 more part,
 And O, while I tell it to you,
It is peace to my soul, it is joy to my heart,
 That old, old story is true.

 That old, old story is true,
 That old, old story is true;
It is peace to my soul, it is joy to my heart,
 That old, old story is true.

4.
O that wonderful story I love to repeat,
 Of peace and good will to men;
There's no story to me that is half so sweet,
 As I hear it again and again.
He invites you to come—He will freely receive,
 And this message He sendeth to you,
"There's a mansion in glory for all who be-
 lieve,"
 That old, old story is true.

 That old, old story is true,
 That old, old story is true;
"There's a mansion in glory for all who believe,'
 That old, old story is true.

175   Marching to the Land Above.

Mrs. W. W. SAVAGE.   J. H. FILLMORE.

Voices in Unison.

1. We are marching to the land a-bove, Beau-ti-ful land a-bove, beau-ti-ful
2. We are marching to the cit - y fair, Beau-ti-ful cit - y fair, beau-ti-ful
3. We are marching to the home of love, Beau-ti-ful home of love, beau-ti-ful

land a-bove; To the land where dwells e-ter - nal love, The beau-ti-ful land a-bove.
cit - y fair; Where the an-gel-anthems fill the air, The beau-ti-ful cit - y fair.
home of love; And our guide-book is the word of God, The beau-ti-ful word of God.

Bass & Tenor. *Voices in Unison.*

And we sing a glad tri - umph-ant song, March-ing a - long, marching a-

long, marching a - long; While our glo-rious Cap-tain leads us on, Marching a-

Chorus. *All voices in Unison.*

long, marching a - long, marching a - long.

1. We are march-ing to the
2. We are march-ing to the
3. We are march-ing to the

Marching to the Land Above.—Concluded.

land a - bove,   Beau-ti - ful land a - bove,   Beau-ti - ful land a - bove; To   a
cit - y fair,   Beau-ti - ful cit - y fair,   Beau-ti - ful cit - y fair; Where the
home of love,   Beau-ti - ful home of love,   Beau-ti - ful home of love; And our

land where dwells e - ter - nal love,   Beau-ti - ful land a - bove,   land a bove.
an - gel - an - thems fill the air,   Beau-ti - ful cit - y fair,   cit - y fair.
guide-book is the word of God,   Beau-ti - ful word of God,   word of God.

176   Rock of Ages.

A. M. TOPLADY.   (TOPLADY. 7s, 6 lines.)   DR. THOS. HASTINGS.

FINE.

1. Rock of A - ges, cleft for me, Let me hide my - self in Thee;
D.C.—Be of sin the doub - le cure; Save me from its guilt and pow'r.

D. C.

Let the wa - ter and the blood, From Thy riv - en side which flow'd,

2 Not the labor of my hands
Can fulfil Thy law's demands;
Could my zeal no respite know,
Could my tears forever flow,
All for sin could not atone;
Thou must save, and Thou alone.

3 Nothing in my hand I bring,
Simply to Thy cross I cling;
Naked, come to Thee for dress,

Helpless, look to Thee for grace;
Foul, I to the fountain fly,
Wash me, Saviour, or I die.

4 While I draw this fleeting breath,
When mine eyes shall close in death,
When I soar to worlds unknown,
See Thee on Thy judgment throne,—
Rock of Ages, cleft for me,
Let me hide myself in Thee.

177 Scatter Seeds of Kindness.

Mrs. A. Smith, alt.   S. J. Vail.

1. Let us gath-er up the sun-beams, Ly-ing all a-round our path;
2. Strange, we nev-er prize the mu-sic Till the sweet-voiced bird is flown;
3. There are vines that now are droop-ing In the cold and chil-ly blast;
4. There is mag-ic in a whis-per, There is mu-sic in a voice,

Let us keep the wheat and ros-es, Cast-ing out the thorns and chaff.
Strange that we should slight the vi-olets Till the love-ly flow'rs are gone!
Let us bind the brok-en ten-trils We, un-heed-ing, oft have passed;
That in tones of love and kind-ness Bid the wea-ry ones re-joice;

Let us find our sweet-est com-fort In the bless-ings of to-day,
Strange that sum-mer skies and sun-shine Nev-er seem one half so fair,
In the sum-mer of the pres-ent, And the sun-shine of to-day,
Heav-y tri-als have been light-ened In the dark and lone-ly hour,

With a pa-tient hand re-mov-ing All the bri-ars from the way.
As when win-ter's snow-y pin-ions Shake the white down in the air.
For the sad and bro-ken-heart-ed, Let us watch and work and pray.
And the burdened souls of ma-ny Have been res-cued by their pow'r.

Chorus.

Then scat-ter seeds of kind-ness, Then scat-ter seeds of kind-ness,

Scatter Seeds of Kindness.—Concluded.

ad lib.

Then scat-ter seeds of kind-ness, For our reap-ing by and by.

178   A Soldier of the Cross.

Isaac Watts.   Ira D. Sankey.

1. Am I a sol - dier of the cross—A fol - l'wer of the Lamb!
2. Must I be car - ried to the skies, On flow - ery beds of ease,
3. Are there no foes for me to face? Must I not stem the flood?
4. Since I must fight if I would reign, In - crease my cour - age, Lord!

And shall I fear to own His cause, Or blush to speak His name?
While oth - ers fought to win the prize, And sailed thro' blood - y seas?
Is this vile world a friend to grace, To help me on to God?
I'll bear the toil, en - dure the pain, Sup - port - ed by Thy word.

Chorus.

In the name.......... of Christ the King,   Who hath purchas'd
          In the name   of Christ the King,

life for me, Thro' grace I'll win the promised crown, What e'er my cross may be.

179

179 Throw Out the Life-Line.

Rev. E. S. Ufford.   E. S. Ufford. Arr. by Geo. C. Stebbins.

1. Throw out the Life-Line a - cross the dark wave, There is a broth-er whom
2. Throw out the Life-Line with hand quick and strong: Why do you tar-ry, why
3. Throw out the Life-Line to dan-ger-fraught men, Sink-ing in an-guish where
4. Soon will the sea-son of res-cue be o'er, Soon will they drift to e-

some one should save; Some-bod-y's broth-er! oh, who then, will dare To
lin - ger, so long? See! he is sink-ing; oh, hast-en to - day— And
you've nev - er been: Winds of temp-ta - tion and bil-lows of woe Will
ter ni - ty's shore, Haste then, my broth-er, no time for de - lay, But

Chorus.

throw out the Life-Line, his per - il to share?
out with the Life-Boat! a - way, then, a - way!
soon hurl them out where the dark wa - ters flow. } Throw out the Life-Line!
throw out the Life-Line and save them to - day.

Throw out the Life-Line! Some one is drift-ing a - way; Throw out the

Life-Line! Throw out the Life-Line! Some one is sink-ing to - day.

180

180 At the Cross.

Isaac Watts. R. E. Hudson.

1. A - las! and did my Sav - iour bleed, And did my Sovereign die?
2. Was it for crimes that I have done, He groaned up - on the tree!
3. But drops of grief can ne'er re - pay The debt of love I owe;

Would He de - vote that sa - cred head For such a worm as I?
A - maz - ing pit - y, grace un - known, And love be - yond de - gree!
Here, Lord, I give my - self a - way, 'Tis all that I can do!

Chorus.

At the cross, at the cross, where I first saw the light, And the

bur - den of my heart rolled a - way, It was there by faith

rolled a - way,

I re - ceived my sight, And now I am hap - py all the day

185

181 For Christ and the Church.

E. E. Hewitt.   [THIRD TUNE.]   Wm. J. Kirkpatrick.

1. "For Christ and the church," let our voic - es ring, Let us hon - or the
2. "For Christ and the church," be our ear - nest pray'r, Let us fol - low His
3. "For Christ and the church," will-ing of - f'rings make, Time and tal - ents and
4. "For Christ and the church," let us cast a - side, By His con - quer-ing

name of our own bless ed King, Let us work with a will in the
ban - ner, the cross dai - ly bear; Let us yield, whol - ly yield, to the
gold, for the dear Mas - ter's sake; We will ren - der the best we can
grace, chains of self, fear and pride; May our lives be en - riched by an

strength of youth, And loy - al - ly stand for the king - dom of truth.
Spir - it's pow'r, And faith - ful - ly serve Him in life's bright est hour.
bring to Him, The heart's wealth of love, that will nev - er grow dim.
aim so grand; Then hap - py the call to the Sav - iour's right hand.

Chorus.

For Christ,.... our dear Re - deem - er, For Christ.... who died to save;
For Christ   For Christ

For the Church..... His blood hath purchased, Lord, make us pure and brave.
For the Church His

My Ain Countrie.

MARY LEE DEMAREST.

IONE T. HANNA. 1861.
Har. by H. P. MAIN.

Additional words and arr. Copyright, 1881, by Biglow & Main.

3 Sae little noo I ken, o' yon blessèd, bonnie place,
I only ken it's Hame, whaur we shall see His face;
It wad surely be eneuch for ever mair to be
In the glory o' His presence, in oor ain countrie.
Like a bairn to his mither, a wee birdie to its nest,
I wad fain be gangin' noo, unto my Saviour's breast,
For He gathers in His bosom witless, worthless lambs like me,
An' carries them Himsel' to His ain countrie.

4 He is faithfu' that hath promised, an' He'll surely come again,
He'll keep His tryst wi' me, at what oor I dinna ken;
But He bids me still to wait, an' ready aye to be,
To gang at ony moment to my ain countrie.
Sae i'm watchin', aye, an' singin' o' my hame, as I wait
For the soun'in' o' His fitfa' this side the gowden gate;
God gie His grace to ilka ane wha' listens noo to me,
That we a' may gang in gladness to oor ain countrie.

183   What a Wonderful Saviour!

E. A. H.

ELISHA A. HOFFMAN.

1. Christ has for sin a-tone-ment made, What a won - der - ful Sav - iour!
2. I'll praise Him for the cleansing blood,— What a won - der - ful Sav - iour!
3. He cleansed my heart from all its sin, What a won - der - ful Sav - iour!
4. He walks be - side me in the way, What a won - der - ful Sav - iour!
5. He gives me o - ver - com-ing pow'r, What a won - der - ful Sav - iour!
6. To Him I've giv - en all my heart, What a won - der - ful Sav - iour!

We are redeemed! the price is paid! What a won - der - ful Sav - iour!
That rec - on - ciled my soul to God; What a won - der - ful Sav - iour!
And now He reigns and rules there-in; What a won - der - ful Sav - iour!
And keeps me faith - ful day by day; What a won - der - ful Sav - iour!
And tri - umph in each try - ing hour; What a won - der - ful Sav - iour!
The world shall nev - er share a part; What a won - der - ful Sav - iour!

Chorus.

What a won - der - ful Sav - iour is Je - sus, my Je - sus!

What a won - der - ful Sav - iour is Je - sus, my Lord!

184 The Lord watch between Me and Thee.

Gen. 31 : 49.   (C. E. BENEDICTION.)   W. H. DOANE.

The Lord watch be - tween me and thee (me and thee), The Lord watch be -

   184

The Lord watch between Me.—Concluded.

tween me and thee (me and thee), The Lord watch be tween me and

rit.

thee (me and thee), When we are ab - sent one from an - oth - er. A - men.

185   Come, Thou Almighty King.

C. WESLEY.   (ITALIAN HYMN. 6, 4.)   FELICE GIARDINI.

1. Come, Thou al - might - y King, Help us Thy name to sing,
2. Come, Thou in - car - nate Word, Gird on Thy might - y sword;
3. Come, Ho - ly Com - fort - er! Thy sa - cred wit - ness bear,
4. To the great One in Three, The high - est prais - es be,

Help us to praise: Fa - ther! all glo - ri - ous, O'er all vic -
Our pray'r at - tend: Come, and Thy peo - ple bless, And give Thy
In this glad hour! Thou, who al - might - y art, Now rule in
Hence ev - er - more! His sov - 'reign maj - es - ty May we in

to - ri - ous, Come, and reign o - ver us, An - cient of Days!
word suc - cess; Spir - it of ho - li - ness! On us de - scend.
ev - 'ry heart, And ne'er from us de - part, Spir - it of pow'r!
glo - ry see, And to e - ter - ni - ty Love and a - dore.

186   We Shall Meet By and By.

JOHN ATKINSON, D.D.

HUBERT P. MAIN.

1. We shall meet be-yond the riv-er, By and by, by and by; And the darkness
2. We shall strike the harps of glo-ry, By and by, by and by; We shall sing re-
3. We shall see and be like Je-sus, By and by, by and by; Who a crown of
4. There our tears shall all cease flowing, By and by, by and by; And with sweetest

shall be o-ver, By and by, by and by; With the toil some jour-ney done,
demption's sto-ry, By and by, by and by; And the strains for ev-er more
life will give us, By and by, by and by; And the an-gels who ful-fil
rapt-ure knowing, By and by, by and by; All the blest ones, who have gone

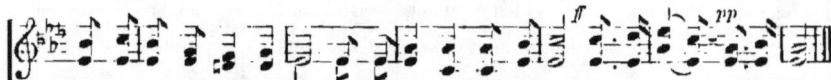

And the glorious bat-tle won, We shall shine forth as the sun, By and by, by and by.
Shall resound in sweetness o'er Yonder ev-er-lasting shore, By and by, by and by.
All the mandates of His will Shall attend, and love us still, By and by, by and by.
To the land of life and song,—We with shoutings shall rejoin, By and by, by and by.

Copyright, 1869, by Hubert P. Main.

187   My Country, 'tis of Thee.

S. F. SMITH, D.D.   (AMERICA. 6, 4.)   H. CAREY.

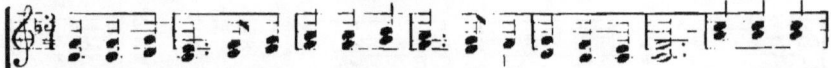

1. My country, 'tis of thee, Sweet land of lib-er-ty, Of thee I sing; Land where my
2. My na-tive country, thee, Land of the no-ble free, Thy name I love; I love thy
3. Let music swell the breeze, And ring from all the trees, Sweet freedom's song; Let mortal
4. Our father's God, to Thee, Au-thor of lib-er-ty, To Thee we sing; Long may our

186

My Country, 'tis of Thee.—Concluded.

fathers died .Land of the pilgrim's pride, From ev-ery mountain side, Let freedom ring.
rocks and rills, Thy woods and templed hills, My heart with rapture thrills, Like that above,
tongues awake, Let all that breathe partake, Let rocks their silence break, The sound prolong.
land be bright, With freedom's ho - ly light, Protect us by Thy might, Great God! our King.

---

188   Just as I Am.

CHARLOTTE ELLIOTT.   (HURSLEY. L. M.)   P. RITTER.

1. Just as I am—with-out one plea, But that Thy blood was shed for me,
2. Just as I am—and wait-ing not, To rid my soul of one dark blot,
3. Just as I am—though toss'd a-bout With many a con - flict, many a doubt,
4. Just as I am—poor, wretched, blind;—Sight, rich-es, heal - ing of the mind,

And that Thou bidd'st me come to Thee, O Lamb of God, I come, I come!
To Thee whose blood can cleanse, each spot, O Lamb of God, I come, I come!
Fightings and fears, with-in, with - out, O Lamb of God, I come, I come!
Yea, all I need, in Thee to find, O Lamb of God, I come, I come!

5 Just as I am—Thou wilt receive,
Wilt welcome, pardon, cleanse, relieve,
Because Thy promise I believe:
   O Lamb of God, I come!

6 Just as I am—Thy love unknown
Hath broken every barrier down;
Now to be Thine, yea, Thine alone,
   O Lamb of God, I come!

---

189   Sun of My Soul.

(Tune—HURSLEY. L. M.)

1 Sun of my soul! Thou Saviour dear,
It is not night if Thou be near:
O, may no earth-born cloud arise
To hide Thee from Thy servant's eyes.

2 When the soft dews of kindly sleep
My wearied eyelids gently steep
Be my last thought, how sweet to rest
Forever on my Saviour's breast!

3 Abide with me from morn till eve,
For without Thee I cannot live;
Abide with me when night is nigh,
For without Thee I dare not die.

4 Come near to bless me when I wake,
Ere through the world my way I take;
Abide with me till in Thy love
I lose myself in heaven above.
                J. KEBLE.

How Firm a Foundation.

G. KEITH.   (PORTUGUESE. 11s.)   M. PORTOGALLO.

1. How firm a foun-da-tion, ye saints of the Lord, Is laid for your faith in His
2. "Fear not, I am with thee, oh, be not dis-mayed, For I am thy God, I will
3. "When thro' the deep wa-ters I call thee to go, The riv-ers of sor-row shall
4. "The soul that on Je-sus hath leaned for re-pose, I will not—I will not de-

ex - cel-lent word! What more can He say, than to you He hath said,— To you, who for
still give thee aid ; I'll strengthen thee,help thee,and cause thee to stand. Up-held by My
not o - ver flow; For I will be with thee thy trouble to bless, And sancti-fy
sert to His foes; That soul—tho' all hell should en-deavor to shake, I'll nev-er—no,

ref' - uge to Je - sus have fled? To you, who for ref - uge to Je - sus have fled?
gracious, om - nip - o - tent hand, Up held by My gra-cious om-nip - o - tent hand.
to thee thy deep-est dis-tress, And sanc-ti - fy to thee thy deep-est dis-tress."
nev - er—no, nev - er for-sake! I'll nev - er—no, nev - er—no, nev - er for - sake!"

191   My Faith Looks Up to Thee.

RAY PALMER.   (OLIVET. 6s, 4s.)   LOWELL MASON.

1. My faith looks up to Thee, Thou Lamb of Cal - va - ry, Sav - iour di - vine!
2. May Thy rich grace im - part Strength to my faint - ing heart; My zeal in - spire;
3. While life's dark maze I tread, And griefs a - round me spread, Be Thou my guide;

My Faith Looks Up to Thee.—Concluded.

Now hear me while I pray. Take all my guilt a - way. Oh. let me
As Thou hast died for me, Oh, may my love to Thee Pure warm, and
Bid dark - ness turn to day, Wipe sor - row's tears a - way, Nor let me

from this day Be whol - ly Thine!
changeless be, A liv - ing fire!
ev - er stray, From Thee a - side.

4.
When ends life's transient dream,
When death's cold sullen stream
   Shall o'er me roll,
Blest Saviour! then, in love,
Fear and distrust remove;
Oh, bear me safe above,
   A ransomed soul!

192   Joy to the World.

Isaac Watts.   (ANTIOCH. C. M.)   Arr from Geo. F. Handel.

1. Joy to the world; the Lord is come! Let earth re - ceive her King;
2. Joy to the earth; the Sav - iour reigns; Let men their songs em - ploy;
3. No more let sins and sor - rows grow, Nor thorns in - fest the ground;
4. He rules the world with truth and grace, And makes the na - tions prove

Let ev - ery heart pre - pare him room, And heav'n and na-ture sing,   And
While fields and floods, rocks, hills, and plains, Re - peat the sound-ing joy &c.
He comes to make his bless ings flow For as the curse is found, &c.
The glo - ries of .... his right cons-ness, And won-ders of his love. &c.
    1. And heav'n,   And heav'n and na ture

heav'n and na ture sing, ... And heav'n, And heav'n and na ture sing.
sing,   And heav'n and na - ture sing

193 Christ Returneth.

H. L. TURNER.

JAMES McGRANAHAN.

1 It may be at morn, when the day is a - wak - ing, When sunlight thro'
2. It may be at mid - day, it may be at twi - light, It may be, per -
3. While hosts cry Ho - san - na, from heav'n de - scending, With glo - ri - fied
4. Oh, joy! oh, de - light! should we go with - out dy - ing, No sick - ness, no

dark - ness and shad - ow is break - ing, That Je - sus will come in the
chance, that the black - ness of mid - night Will burst in - to light in the
saints and the an - gels at - tend - ing, With grace on His brow, like a
sad - ness, no dread and no cry - ing, Caught up thro' the clouds with our

full - ness of glo - ry, To re - ceive from the world "His own."
blaze of His glo - ry, When.. Je - sus re - ceives "His own."
ha - lo of glo - ry, Will.... Je - sus re - ceive "His own."
Lord in - to glo - ry, When.. Je - sus re - ceives "His own."

Chorus.

O Lord Je - sus, how long, how long Ere we shout the glad song, Christ re -

rit.

turn - eth; Hal - le - lu - jah! hal - le - lu - jah! A - men, Hal - le - lu - jah! A - men.

194 The Cleansing Fountain.

Rev. F. BOTTOME. by per.   S. J. VAIL.

1. Be - neath the glo - rious throne a - bove, The crys - tal fount - ain spring-ing,
2. Thro' all my soul its wa - ters flow, Thro' all my na - ture steal - ing;
3. The bar - ren wastes are fruit - ful lands, The des - ert blooms with ro - ses;
4. Oh, depth of mer - cy! breadth of grace! Oh, love of God un - bound - ed!

A riv - er, full of life and love, Is joy and glad - ness bring - ing.
And deep with - in my heart I know The con - scious-ness of heal - ing.
And He, the glo - ry of all lands, His love - ly face dis - clos - es.
My soul is lost in sweet a - maze, By won - drous love con - found - ed!

Chorus.

O Fount of cleans-ing, flow-ing free! That Fount is o - pened wide for me;

For me, ... for me, ... is o - pened wide for me.....
For me, for me,

By per. The Biglow & Main Co., owners of Copyright.

195 Gloria Patri.

Glory be to the Father, and to the Son, and to the Ho - ly Ghost.
As it was in the beginning,
is now, and .... ev - er shall be, world with - out end. A - MEN.

196 The Palace of the King.

Psalm 45:10-17.   (Metrical Version.)   Dr. J. B. Herbert.

1. O daugh-ter take good heed, In-cline, and give good ear; Thou must for-
2. The daugh-ter then of Tyre, There with a gift shall be, And all the
3. She com-eth to the King In robes with nee-dle wrought; The vir-gins
4. And in thy fa-ther's stead, Thy chil-dren thou shalt take, And in all

get thy kin-dred all, And fa-ther's house most dear. Thy beau-ty to the
wealth-y of the land Shall make their suit to thee. The daughter of the
that do fol-low her Shall un-to thee be brought. With gladness and with
plac-es of the earth Them no-ble prin-ces make. I will show forth thy

King, Shall then de-light-ful be; And do thou hum-bly wor-ship Him, Be-
King, All-glo-rious is with-in; And with em-broid-er-ies of gold Her
joy, Thou all of them shall bring, And they to-geth-er en-ter shall The
name To gen-er-a-tions all: The peo-ple there-fore ev-er-more To

Chorus.

cause thy Lord is He. }
garments wrought have been. } With gladness and with Joy, Thou all of them shalt
pal-ace of the King. }
thee give prais-es shall. }

bring, And they to-geth-er en-ter shall The pal-ace of the King,

The Palace of the King.—Concluded.

The pal-ace of the King, The pal-ace of the King; And

they to-geth-er en-ter shall The pal-ace of the King.

rit.

197   How Blest the Man.

Psalm 1.   (Metrical Version.)   D. BORTNIANSKI.

1. How blest the man that doth not stray Where wick-ed coun-sel tempts his feet;
2. He shall be like the tree that springs Where streams of wa-ter gen-tly glide;
3. Not so un-god-ly men, for they Like chaff be-fore the wind are driven;

Who stands not in the sin-ner's way, And sits not in the scorn-er's seat,
Which plen-teous fruit in sea-son brings, And ev-er green its leaves a-bide;
Hence they'll not stand in judg-ment day, Nor min-gle with the saints in heav'n:

But in God's law he takes de-light, And med-i-tates both day and night.
Thus shall pros-per-i-ty at-tend The good man's work till life shall end.
The Lord ap-proves the good man's path, But sin-ner's ways shall end in wrath.

198   Good is Jehovah the Lord.

Psalm 100.   (Metrical Version.)   JAMES McGRANAHAN.

1. All peo - ple that dwell on the earth, Your songs to Je - ho - vah now raise;
2. Know ye that Je - ho - vah is God, Our Sov-'reign and Mak er is He,
3. O en - ter His tem - ple with praise, His por - tals with thankful ac - claim;

O wor ship Je - ho - vah with mirth, A - proach Him with an-thems of praise.
His peo - ple who bow to His rod, And sheep of His pas-ture are we.
Your voic - es in thanks-giv-ing raise, And bless ye His glo - ri - ous name.

Chorus.

For good is Je - ho - vah the Lord, His mer - cy to
Je - ho - vah the Lord,

us nev - er ends (nev - er ends ; His faith - ful - ness true to His

word (to His word), Thro' a - ges un - end - ing ex - tends.

199

O Whither?

(Metrical Version.)

Psalm 139.   Dr. J. B. HERBERT.

1. Lord, Thou hast search'd me, and hast known My ris - ing up and lay - ing down,
2. Thou know'st my path and ly - ing down, And all my ways to Thee are known;
3. Be - hind, be - fore me, Thou dost stand, And lay on me Thy might - y hand;

And from a far Thy search-ing eye Be - holds my tho'ts that se - cret lie.
For in my tongue no word can be, But, lo, O Lord, 'tis known to Thee.
Such knowledge is for me too strange, 'Tis high be - yond my ut - most range.

Chorus.

Whith - er, whith - er shall my foot steps fly, Be - yond the Spir - it's searching eye?

O whither, whither shall my foot steps fly, Beyond Thy Spir - it's searching eye?

4 O whither shall my footsteps fly,
  Beyond Thy Spirit's searching eye?
  To what retreat shall I repair,
  And find not Thy dread presence there?

5 If I to heaven shall ascend,
  Thy presence there will me attend;
  If in the grave I make my bed,
  Lo, there I find Thy presence dread.

6 If on the morning wings I flee,
  And dwell in utmost parts of the sea;

Even there Thy hand shall guide my way,
And Thy right hand shall be my stay.

7 Or, if I say, to shun Thine eye,
  In shades of darkness I will lie,
  Around me then the very night
  Will shine as shines the noon-day light.

8 From Thee the shades can nought disguise,
  The night is day before Thine eyes;
  The darkness is to Thee as bright
  As are the beams of noon-day light.

200   Who is on the Lord's Side?

F. R. HAVERGAL, by per.

IRA D. SANKEY.

Spirited.

1. Who is on the Lord's side? Who will serve the King? Who will be His help-ers,
2. Now for weight of glo-ry, Not for crown and palm, En-ter we the ar-my,
3. Je-sus, Thou hast bought us, Not with gold or gem, But with Thine own life-blood,
4. Fierce may be the con-flict, Strong may be the foe, But the King's own ar-my,

Oth-er lives to bring? Who will leave the world's side? Who will face the foe?
Raise the war rior-psalm: But for Him who claim-eth Lives for Him who died,
For Thy di-a-dem; With Thy bless-ing fill-ing All who come to Thee,
None can o-ver-throw; Round His standard rang-ing, Vic-t'ry is se-cure,

Who is on the Lord's side? Who for Him will go?
He whom Je-sus nam-eth Must be on His side.
Thou hast made us will-ing, Thou hast made us free.
For His truth un-chang-ing Makes the triumph sure.

Chorus.

} Who is on the Lord's side?

Who will serve the King? Who will be His help-ers, Oth-er lives to bring? By Thy

grand redemption, By Thy grace di-vine, We are on the Lord's side; Saviour, we are Thine.

Copyright, 1881, by Ira D. Sankey.

201 God be with You!

J. E. RANKIN, D.D.   W. G. TOMER.

1. God be with you till we meet a - gain!— By His coun-sels guide, up-
2. God be with you till we meet a - gain!— 'Neath His wings pro-tect-ing
3. God be with you till we meet a - gain!— When life's per-ils thick con-
4. God be with you till we meet a - gain!— Keep love's ban-ner float-ing

hold you, With His sheep se - cure - ly fold you; God
hide you, Dai - ly man - na still di - vide you; God be
found you, Put His arms un - fail - ing 'round you; God be
o'er you, Smite death's threat'ning wave be - fore you; God be

Chorus.

with you till we meet a - gain!) Till we meet!.......... Till we
with you till we meet a - gain!)
with you till we meet a - gain!) Till we meet! till we
with you till we meet a - gain!)

meet! Till we meet at Je - sus' feet; Till we
meet a - gain! Till we meet!

meet!........ Till we meet! God be with you till we meet a - gain!
Till we meet! till we meet a - gain!

By per. Rev. J. E. Rankin, owner of Copyright.

Gospel Hymns.

202   Tune, 222.   G. H. Consolidated.

1 Holy, holy, holy;   Lord God Almighty!
  Early in the morning our song shall rise to
      Thee!
  Holy, holy, holy! Merciful and Mighty!
  God in Three Persons, blessed Trinity!

2 Holy, holy, holy! all the saints adore Thee,
  Casting down their golden crowns around the
      glassy sea;
  Cherubim and seraphim falling down before
      Thee,
  Which wert, and art, and evermore shalt be.

3 Holy, holy, holy! Lord God Almighty!
  All Thy works shall praise Thy name in
      earth, and sky, and sea;
  Holy, holy, holy! Merciful and Mighty!
  God in Three Persons, blessed Trinity! Amen.

203   Tune, 193.   G. H. No. 5.

1 Sowing in the morning, sowing seeds of kind-
      ness,
  Sowing in the noon-tide and the dewy eve;
  Waiting for the harvest, and the time of
      reaping,   [sheaves.
  We shall come, rejoicing, bringing in the
Cho.—Bringing in the sheaves! bringing in the
          sheaves!   [sheaves.
  We shall come, rejoicing, bringing in the

2 Sowing in the sunshine, sowing in the shad-
      ows,   [breeze;
  Fearing neither clouds nor winter's chilling
  By and by the harvest, and the labor ended,
  We shall come, rejoicing, bringing in the
      sheaves.

3 Going forth with weeping, sowing for the
      Master,   [grieves;
  Though the loss sustained, our spirit often
  When our weeping's over, He will bid us
      welcome,   [sheaves.
  We shall come, rejoicing, bringing in the

204   Tune, 249. C. E. Ed.   G. H. No. 6.

1 A Christian band from far and near,
  We meet to learn of Jesus here,
  To read His word, whose every line
  Is full of hope and joy divine.
Cho.—This blest Endeavor band,
      From o'er all this broad land,
      Is gathered in His name,
      To grasp the friendly hand;
      Our thoughts are one in Thee,
      Our prayer shall ever be,
      That God may bless and (ever) keep
      This Christian band. (The Y. P. S. C. E.)

2 A Christian band where all may sing
  Glad songs of praise to God our King;
  And youthful hearts may find the way
  To perfect peace and endless day.

3 Each willing hand and thankful heart,
  Is bound again before we part,
  As sheaves on earth are bound with twine,
  His word shall bind as cords divine.

4 The Master's work we'll still pursue,
  And once again our pledge renew,
  To Him who saves us by His love,
  Till gathered home with Him above.

205   Tune, 151.   G. H. No. 5.

1 Come, ye that love the Lord,
  And let your joys be known,
  Join in a song with sweet accord
  And thus surround the throne.
Cho.—We're marching to Zion,
      Beautiful, beautiful Zion;
      We're marching upward to Zion,
      The beautiful city of God.

2 Let those refuse to sing
  Who never knew our God;
  But children of the heav'nly King
  May speak their joys abroad.

3 The hill of Zion yields
  A thousand sacred sweets,
  Before we reach the heav'nly fields,
  Or walk the golden streets.

4 Then let our songs abound,
  And ev'ry tear be dry;
  We're marching thro' Immanuel's ground,
  To fairer worlds on high.

206   Tune, 204.   G. H. No. 6.

1 I hear Thy welcome voice
  That calls me, Lord, to Thee,
  For cleansing in Thy precious blood
  That flowed on Calvary.
Cho.—I am coming, Lord!
      Coming now to Thee!
      Wash me, cleanse me in the blood
      That flowed on Calvary.

2 Tho' coming weak and vile,
  Thou dost my strength assure;
  Thou dost my vileness fully cleanse,
  Till spotless all and pure.

3 'Tis Jesus calls me on
  To perfect faith and love;
  To perfect hope, and peace, and trust,
  For earth and heaven above.

4 'Tis Jesus who confirms
  The blessed work within,
  By adding grace to welcomed grace,
  Where reigned the power of sin.

207   Tune, 188.   G. H. No. 6.

1 My hope is built on nothing less
  Than Jesus' blood and righteousness;
  I dare not trust the sweetest frame,
  But wholly lean on Jesus' name.
Cho.—On Christ the solid rock I stand;
      All other ground is sinking sand.

2 When darkness veils His lovely face,
  I rest on His unchanging grace;
  In every high and stormy gale,
  My anchor holds within the veil.

3 His oath, His covenant, His blood,
  Support me in the whelming flood:
  When all around my soul gives way,
  He then is all my hope and stay.

4 When He shall come with trumpet sound,
  O, may I then in Him be found,
  Drest in His righteousness alone,
  Faultless to stand before the throne!

Gospel Hymns.

208 Tune, 165. G. H. No. 5.

1 Simply trusting every day,
Trusting thro' a stormy way;
Even when my faith is small,
Trusting Jesus, that is all.

Cho.—Trusting as the moments fly,
Trusting as the days go by;
Trusting Him whate'er befall,
Trusting Jesus, that is all.

2 Brightly doth His Spirit shine
Into this poor heart of mine;
While He leads I cannot fall;
Trusting Jesus, that is all.

3 Singing, if my way is clear;
Praying, if the path is drear;
If in danger, for Him call;
Trusting Jesus, that is all.

4 Trusting Him while life shall last,
Trusting Him till earth be past;
Till within the jasper wall,
Trusting Jesus, that is all.

---

209 Tune, 180. G. H. No. 5.

1 'Tis the blessed hour of prayer, when our
hearts lowly bend,   [Friend;
And we gather to Jesus our Saviour and
If we come to Him in faith, His protection to
share.   [be there!
What a balm for the weary! oh, how sweet to

Cho.—Blessed hour of pray'r, Blessed hour of
pray'r,
What a balm for the weary! oh, how
sweet to be there!

2 'Tis the blessed hour of prayer, when the
Saviour draws near,   [hear;
With a tender compassion His children to
When He tells us we may cast at His feet every
care;   [be there!
What a balm for the weary! oh, how sweet to

3 'Tis the blessed hour of prayer when the
tempted and tried   [confide;
To the Saviour who loves them their sorrow
With a sympathizing heart He removes every
care;   [be there!
What a balm for the weary! oh, how sweet to

---

210 Tune, 170. G. H. No. 5.

1 My Jesus, I love Thee, I know Thou art mine!
For Thee all the follies of sin I resign;
My gracious Redeemer, my Saviour art Thou!
If ever I loved Thee, my Jesus, 'tis now.

2 I love Thee, because Thou hast first loved
me,
And purchased my pardon on Calvary's tree;
I love Thee for wearing the thorns on Thy
brow;
If ever I loved Thee, my Jesus, 'tis now.

3 I will love Thee in life, I will love Thee in
death,
And praise Thee as long as Thou lendest me
breath;
And say when the death-dew lies cold on my
brow,
"If ever I loved Thee, my Jesus, 'tis now."

211 Tune, 176. G. H. No. 5.

1 Rescue the perishing,
Care for the dying,
Snatch them in pity from sin and the grave;
Weep o'er the erring one,
Lift up the fallen,
Tell them of Jesus, the Mighty to save.

Cho.—Rescue the perishing,
Care for the dying;
Jesus is merciful,
Jesus will save.

2 Though they are slighting Him,
Still He is waiting,
Waiting the penitent child to receive;
Plead with them earnestly,
Plead with them gently;
He will forgive if they only believe.

3 Down in the human heart,
Crushed by the tempter,
Feelings lie buried that grace can restore;
Touched by a loving heart,
Wakened by kindness,   [more.
Chords that were broken will vibrate once

4 Rescue the perishing,
Duty demands it;
Strength for thy labor the Lord will provide;
Back to the narrow way
Patiently win them;
Tell the poor wanderer a Saviour has died.

---

212 Tune, 166. G. H. No. 5.

1 Yield not to temptation,
For yielding is sin.
Each victory will help you
Some other to win,
Fight manfully onward,
Dark passions subdue,
Look ever to Jesus,
He'll carry you through.

Cho.—Ask the Saviour to help you,
Comfort, strengthen and keep you:
He is willing to aid you,
He will carry you through.

2 Shun evil companions,
Bad language disdain;
God's name hold in rev'rence,
Nor take it in vain:
Be thoughtful and earnest,
Kind-hearted and true,
Look ever to Jesus,
He'll carry you through.

3 To him that o'ercometh
God giveth a crown,
Thro' faith we shall conquer,
Though often cast down;
He, who is our Saviour,
Our strength will renew;
Look ever to Jesus,
He'll carry you through.

---

213 TEMPERANCE DOXOLOGY.
Tune, Old Hundred. No. 105.

Praise God, from whom all blessings flow!
Praise Him, who saves from sin and woe!
Praise Him, who leads the Temperance host!
Praise Father, Son and Holy Ghost.

Gospel Hymns.

214   Tune, EVAN.   No. 143.

1 Come, Holy Spirit, Heavenly Dove!
    With all Thy quick'ning powers;
    Kindle a flame of sacred love
    In these cold hearts of ours.

2 Dear Lord, and shall we ever live
    At this poor dying rate—
    Our love so faint, so cold to Thee,
    And Thine to us so great?

3 Come, Holy Spirit, Heavenly Dove!
    With all Thy quick'ning powers;
    Come, shed abroad a Saviour's Love,
    And that shall kindle ours.

215   Tune, 168.   G. H. No. 6.

1 Sweet hour of prayer! sweet hour of prayer!
    That calls me from a world of care,
    And bids me at my Father's throne
    Make all my wants and wishes known:
    In seasons of distress and grief,
    My soul has often found relief,—
    And oft escaped the tempter's snare,
    By thy return, sweet hour of prayer!

2 Sweet hour of prayer! sweet hour of prayer!
    Thy wings shall my petition bear
    To Him whose truth and faithfulness
    Engage the waiting soul to bless;
    And since He bids me seek His face,
    Believe His word, and trust His grace,
    I'll cast on Him my every care,
    And wait for thee, sweet hour of prayer!

3 Sweet hour of prayer! sweet hour of prayer!
    May I thy consolation share,
    Till, from Mount Pisgah's lofty height,
    I view my home and take my flight;
    This robe of flesh I'll drop, and rise
    To seize the everlasting prize;
    And shout, while passing through the air,
    Farewell, farewell, sweet hour of prayer!

216   Tune, No. 167.   G. H. No. 5.

1 What a Friend we have in Jesus,
    All our sins and griefs to bear!
    What a privilege to carry
    Everything to God in prayer!
    Oh, what peace we often forfeit,
    Oh, what needless pain we bear—
    All because we do not carry
    Everything to God in prayer!

2 Have we trials and temptations?
    Is there trouble anywhere?
    We should never be discouraged;
    Take it to the Lord in prayer.
    Can we find a Friend so faithful,
    Who will all our sorrows share?
    Jesus knows our every weakness—
    Take it to the Lord in prayer.

3 Are we weak and heavy laden,
    Cumbered with a load of care?
    Precious Saviour, still our refuge,—
    Take it to the Lord in prayer—
    Do thy friends despise, forsake thee?
    Take it to the Lord in prayer:
    In His arms He'll take and shield thee,
    Thou wilt find a solace there.

217   Tune, 215.   G. H. No. 6.

1 The Lord's our Rock, in Him we hide,
    A shelter in the time of storm!
    Secure, whatever ill betide;
    A shelter in the time of storm!

Cho.—Oh, Jesus is a Rock in a weary land!
    A weary land, a weary land;
    Oh, Jesus is a Rock in a weary land,—
    A shelter in the time of storm.

2 A shade by day, defence by night;
    A shelter in the time of storm!
    No fears alarm, no foes affright;
    A shelter in the time of storm.

3 The raging storms may round us beat;
    A shelter in the time of storm!
    We'll never leave our safe retreat;
    A shelter in the time of storm.

4 O Rock divine, O Refuge dear;
    A shelter in the time of storm!
    Be Thou our helper ever near;
    A shelter in the time of storm.

218   Tune, 227.   G. H. No. 6.

1 Stand up! stand up for Jesus!
    Ye soldiers of the cross;
    Lift high His royal banner,
    It must not suffer loss;
    From vict'ry unto vict'ry
    His army He shall lead,
    Till every foe is vanquished,
    And Christ is Lord indeed.

2 Stand up! stand up for Jesus!
    The trumpet call obey;
    Forth to the mighty conflict
    In this His glorious day!
    Ye that are men, now serve Him,
    Against unnumbered foes;
    Let courage rise with danger,
    And strength to strength oppose.

3 Stand up! stand up for Jesus!
    Stand in His strength alone;
    The arm of flesh will fail you—
    Ye dare not trust your own!
    Put on the gospel armor,
    And, watching unto prayer,
    Where duty calls, or danger,
    Be never wanting there.

219   Tune, 237.   G. H. 5 & 6 Comb.

1 From Greenland's icy mountains,
    From India's coral strand,
    Where Afric's sunny fountains
    Roll down their golden sand,—
    From many an ancient river,
    From many a palmy plain,
    They call us to deliver
    Their land from error's chain.

2 What though the spicy breezes
    Blow soft o'er Ceylon's isle,
    Though every prospect pleases,
    And only man is vile!
    In vain with lavish kindness,
    The gifts of God are strown;
    The heathen, in his blindness,
    Bows down to wood and stone

Gospel Hymns.

3 Shall we, whose souls are lighted
By wisdom from on high,
Shall we, to men benighted
The lamp of life deny!
Salvation! oh, salvation!
The joyful sound proclaim,
Till earth's remotest nation
Has learned Messiah's name.

220   Tune, 8.   G. H. Consolidated.

1 What means this eager, anxious throng,
Which moves with busy haste along—
These wondrous gatherings day by day?
What means this strange commotion, pray?
In accents hush'd the throng reply,
"Jesus of Nazareth passeth by."

2 Who is this Jesus? Why should He
The city move so mightily?
A passing stranger, has He skill
To move the multitude at will?
Again the stirring notes reply,
"Jesus of Nazareth passeth by."

3 Jesus! 'tis He who once below
Man's pathway trod, 'mid pain and woe;
And burdened ones, where'er He came,
Brought out their sick, and deaf, and lame;
The blind rejoiced to hear the cry:
"Jesus of Nazareth passeth by."

4 Again He comes! From place to place
His holy footprints we can trace.
He pauseth at our threshold—nay,
He enters—condescends to stay;
Shall we not gladly raise the cry?
"Jesus of Nazareth passeth by."

5 Ho! all ye heavy-laden, come!
Here's pardon, comfort, rest, and home;
Ye wanderers from a Father's face,
Return, accept His proffered grace;
Ye tempted ones, there's refuge nigh:
"Jesus of Nazareth passeth by."

6 But if you still His call refuse,
And all His wondrous love abuse,
Soon will He sadly from you turn,
Your bitter prayer for pardon spurn:
"Too late! too late!" will be the cry?—
"Jesus of Nazareth has passed by."

221   Tune, 194.   G. H. No. 6.

1 Saviour, like a Shepherd lead us,
Much we need Thy tend'rest care;
In Thy pleasant pastures feed us,
For our use Thy folds prepare.
Blessed Jesus, Blessed Jesus,
Thou hast bought us, Thine we are.

2 We are Thine, do Thou befriend us,
Be the Guardian of our way;
Keep Thy flock, from sin defend us,
Seek us when we go astray.
Blessed Jesus, Blessed Jesus,
Hear, O hear us, when we pray.

3 Thou hast promised to receive us,
Poor and sinful though we be;
Thou hast mercy to relieve us,
Grace to cleanse, and power to free.
Blessed Jesus, Blessed Jesus,
We will early turn to Thee.

222   Tune, 154.   G. H. No. 5.

1 There were ninety and nine that safely lay
In the shelter of the fold,
But one was out on the hills away,
Far off from the gates of gold—
Away on the mountains wild and bare,
Away from the tender Shepherd's care.

2 "Lord, Thou hast here Thy ninety and nine;
Are they not enough for Thee?"
But the Shepherd made answer: "This of mine
Has wandered away from me,
And, although the road be rough and steep,
I go to the desert to find my sheep."

3 But none of the ransomed ever knew
How deep were the waters crossed;
Nor how dark was the night that the Lord pass'd through
Ere He found His sheep that was lost.
Out in the desert He heard its cry—
Sick, and helpless, and ready to die.

4 "Lord, whence are those blood-drops all the way
That mark out the mountain's track?"
"They were shed for one who had gone astray,
Ere the Shepherd could bring him back."
"Lord, whence are Thy hands so rent and torn?"
"They are pierced to-night by many a thorn."

5 But all thro' the mountains, thunder-riven,
And up from the rocky steep,
There arose a glad cry to the gate of heaven
"Rejoice! I have found my sheep!"
And the angels echoed around the throne,
"Rejoice, for the Lord brings back His own!"

223   Tune, 225.   G. H. No. 6.

1 Work, for the night is coming!
Work through the morning hours;
Work, while the dew is sparkling,
Work, 'mid springing flowers;
Work, when the day grows brighter,
Work, in the glowing sun:
Work, for the night is coming,
When man's work is done.

2 Work, for the night is coming!
Work, through the sunny noon;
Fill brightest hours with labor;
Rest comes sure and soon.
Give every flying minute
Something to keep in store;
Work, for the night is coming,
When man works no more.

3 Work, for the night is coming.
Under the sunset skies!
While their bright tints are glowing,
Work, for daylight flies.
Work, till the last beam fadeth,
Fadeth to shine no more;
Work, while the night is darkening,
When man's work is o'er.

Y. P. S. C. E.

Motto:
"FOR CHRIST AND THE CHURCH."

Active Member's Pledge.

TRUSTING IN THE LORD JESUS CHRIST FOR STRENGTH, I PROMISE HIM THAT I WILL STRIVE TO DO WHATEVER HE WOULD LIKE TO HAVE ME DO; THAT I WILL MAKE IT THE RULE OF MY LIFE TO PRAY AND TO READ THE BIBLE EVERY DAY, AND TO SUPPORT MY OWN CHURCH IN EVERY WAY, ESPECIALLY BY ATTENDING ALL HER REGULAR SUNDAY AND MID-WEEK SERVICES, UNLESS PREVENTED BY SOME REASON WHICH I CAN CONSCIENTIOUSLY GIVE TO MY SAVIOUR; AND THAT, JUST SO FAR AS I KNOW HOW, THROUGHOUT MY WHOLE LIFE, I WILL ENDEAVOR TO LEAD A CHRISTIAN LIFE. AS AN ACTIVE MEMBER I PROMISE TO BE TRUE TO ALL MY DUTIES; TO BE PRESENT AT AND TO TAKE SOME PART, ASIDE FROM SINGING, IN EVERY CHRISTIAN ENDEAVOR PRAYER-MEETING, UNLESS HINDERED BY SOME REASON WHICH I CAN CONSCI-ENTIOUSLY GIVE TO MY LORD AND MASTER. IF OBLIGED TO BE ABSENT FROM THE MONTHLY CONSECRATION-MEETING OF THE SOCIETY, I WILL, IF POSSIBLE, SEND AT LEAST A VERSE OF SCRIPTURE TO BE READ IN RESPONSE TO MY NAME AT THE ROLL-CALL.

Benediction:
"THE LORD WATCH BETWEEN ME AND THEE WHEN WE ARE ABSENT ONE FROM ANOTHER."

TOPICAL INDEX.

A

Topical Index.

A   204

INDEX.

Titles in SMALL CAPITALS; First Lines in Roman.

A
205

Index.

Index.

Index.

A   208

www.ingramcontent.com/pod-product-compliance
Lightning Source LLC
Chambersburg PA
CBHW030827270326
41928CB00007B/928